D1427258

Gustav Jahoda was born in Vienna in 1920, and educated in Vienna, Paris and London. After serving in the Army he became tutor at the Oxford Extra-Mural Delegacy and then lecturer at the University of Manchester. In 1952 he left to take up a teaching and research post at the then University College of the Gold Coast (now University of Ghana). His major field of work at this time, and on several return trips since then, concerned cross-cultural aspects of attitudes, perception and developmental psychology. In the course of this work he came across a number of medicine men and fetish priests, and initial prejudice gave way to a healthy respect for their skill and insight. At the same time it was puzzling to find not only them, but many other western-educated people of high ability and intelligence, firmly maintaining beliefs in witchcraft and sorcery. This led to his developing a more general interest in 'superstition' as a psychological problem. In 1956 he returned to Britain to a post at the University of Glasgow, and in 1964 he moved to a newly established chair at the University of Strathclyde. His other publications include *White Man* (a study of African attitudes to Europeans) and numerous articles on cross-cultural, social and developmental psychology.

Professor Jahoda is married, with four children.

Gustav Jahoda

THE PSYCHOLOGY OF
SUPERSTITION

PENGUIN BOOKS

Penguin Books Ltd, Harmondsworth,
Middlesex, England
Penguin Books Inc., 7110 Ambassador Road,
Baltimore, Maryland 21207, U.S.A.
Penguin Books Australia Ltd, Ringwood,
Victoria, Australia

First published by Allen Lane The Penguin Press 1969
Published in Pelican Books 1970
Copyright © Gustav Jahoda, 1969

Made and printed in Great Britain by
Richard Clay (The Chaucer Press) Ltd, Bungay, Suffolk
Set in Monotype Ehrhardt

For Jean

Contents

CHAPTER ONE

What is Superstition?

It is hard to mark out the boundaries of superstition. A Frenchman travelling in Italy finds almost everything superstitious, and is hardly wrong. The archbishop of Canterbury claims that the archbishop of Paris is superstitious; the Presbyterians levy the same reproach against his Grace of Canterbury, and are in their turn called superstitious by the Quakers, who are the most superstitious of men in the eyes of other Christians.

Voltaire *Philosophical Dictionary*

Many words in everyday use are deceptive. On hearing them, we have the confident feeling that we understand them clearly; but if we were suddenly challenged to define them, we would discover that our certainty was a convenient illusion. Take 'democracy', a word that has nowadays achieved an almost universally favourable connotation; hence most countries tend to claim that they are 'democracies'. Suppose one had to decide whether a particular state is or is not a 'democracy'. The dictionary definition of 'government by the people' is not really much help if one tries to apply it in practice. There are of course lots of criteria one might apply, such as the presence or absence of free elections, the degree of control exercised by the state over the individual, and numerous others. A little closer scrutiny reveals that such criteria themselves tend to be rather ambiguous. How do we assess the degree of control exercised by the state, and at what point does it become excessive by 'democratic' standards? Do 'free' elections require a secret ballot? If so, Britain in mid nineteenth century was not a democracy. Let us ask some concrete questions: are the 'people's democracies' or the new

African one-party states *real* democracies? The answers will depend on the specific set of criteria chosen, the manner in which they are applied and the relative weight attached to each of them; this in turn will be largely determined by the political views of those making the judgements, and thereby the circle is complete. This is not to suggest that the word 'democracy' is meaningless, but only that its meaning is always closely linked to a particular social and political context. Similar considerations apply to 'superstition', and it is therefore no use expecting a precise definition of this term at the outset. However, at least some rough kind of working definition is necessary, and the struggle towards this will be rewarded by a first encounter with some of the subtle problems in which this whole topic is enmeshed.

While it has already been indicated that dictionary definitions are not particularly helpful, they do serve as a convenient starting point. Hence some of those given by the Shorter Oxford Dictionary will be examined, beginning with 'Irrational or unfounded belief in general'. In this widest sense, the label of 'superstition' merely shows that the user wishes to characterize given beliefs or opinions as false. For instance, near the turn of the century a book was published with the title *Studies of Contemporary Superstition*.[1]* Among the 'superstitions' assailed there are the laws on marriage and divorce, Fabian socialism and, curiously enough, T. H. Huxley's agnosticism; with regard to the last the author was so incensed that he described it as 'a superstition more abject more meaningless, and more ridiculous than that of any African, savage, grovelling and mumbling before his fetish'. Used in this way, the term is little more than a verbal bludgeon to trounce one's ideological opponents, much like the practice in South Africa of dubbing as 'communists' any critics of *apartheid*.

Another definition offered by the dictionary is 'an irrational religious belief or practice', and here one runs immediately into the question as to who decides whether a particular belief is irrational. The trouble is that one man's religion is another man's 'superstition'. Missionaries of an earlier age thus labelled the indigenous religions they were trying to supersede. Moreover, as Voltaire suggested, such unflattering descriptions were not

*References are listed at the end of the chapter (p. 16).

unusual even as between different Christian denominations. In one of his letters, Lord Chesterfield observed to his son that he might be surprised to encounter during his travels the absurd superstitions of Papists, explaining that these were due either to ignorance or stupidity. All this is characteristic of the widespread human tendency to denigrate the intellectual status, and often also the motives, of those who disagree with us on an issue we consider important.

So far this study of the dictionary has not been profitable, but there remains one further set of definitions: 'Unreasoning awe or fear of something unknown, mysterious or imaginary; a tenet, scruple, habit etc. founded on fear or ignorance'. Here one seems to be getting nearer the root of the matter, and the first thing to note is the reference to an emotional element. This is an essential attribute of whatever we shall consider to be 'superstition', since it would otherwise fail altogether to affect behaviour, and thus not be very interesting. There are a great variety of beliefs people acquire casually and with practically no emotional investment. For instance, some might believe that cashew nuts grow on trees (which happens to be true) and others may have learnt from the BBC that spaghetti grows on bushes (which happens to be false); neither is likely to have any appreciable influence on behaviour. This is not to say that the emotional component needs to be powerful, only that it ought to be capable of being observed, or inferred to be present in some degree.

The use in these last definitions of the terms 'unreasoning', 'ignorance', 'imaginary', brings one again face to face with the problem of how to decide that these are applied justifiably. Such words are used about beliefs one does not share and which, moreover, one holds in low esteem. In other words, the definition here merely reflects the fact that the term 'superstition' has a strongly pejorative flavour; few people care to admit that they themselves are superstitious. Those in our contemporary society who hold beliefs at variance with what is generally accepted take care to clothe them in positive-sounding verbal garb, calling them 'ancient lore', 'wisdom of the East' or 'occult science'. Frequently they feel themselves to be an enlightened minority, superior in understanding and insight to the rest of us, and they would indignantly reject the idea that they are 'superstitious'. It may be objected that there surely must be ways of deciding who is right, and tough-minded rationalists have suggested some. One of them, Professor A. E. Heath,[2] has formulated the following proposal:

... superstition, whether casual or not, can be treated on objective lines. It is a mathematical matter of the odds for or against. This provides a rough 'ready-reckoner' for assigning beliefs to their proper place on a scale stretching from mere superstition to reasonable expectation. The importance of this is that the method can be applied to religious beliefs in order to judge whether they are superstitions or not. If there is evidence for a belief, if its probabilities are calculable and of reasonable amount, then there is nothing irrational in taking a chance in believing it. But if the odds cannot be estimated, or if they are grossly weighted against what is believed, then the belief is a superstition.

At first sight it might appear that one has here a satisfactory solution to the problem. Let us try and apply it to a particular case, say the Loch Ness monster: is the belief in this a superstition, or is it not? There are numerous eye-witness reports, many of them by persons of unquestioned ability and integrity; the existence of a large animal in Loch Ness has been taken seriously enough to equip and send there expeditions manned by scientifically respectable and well-qualified people; and a film has been taken actually showing the creature swimming along. On the other hand, as will be shown in more detail later, even eye-witness accounts of unusual phenomena are notoriously unreliable; none of the surveys so far has found anything; and many competent zoologists reject the evidence for the monster as weak (the film is open to other interpretations) and put forward several considerations suggesting that the monster is a myth; for instance, unless the creature enjoys an extraordinary longevity, there ought to be at least one whole family of monsters, yet the sightings are comparatively infrequent.

Where, then, does the Loch Ness monster lie on the scale that ranges from mere superstition to reasonable expectation? It will be apparent that there cannot be even a rough-and-ready answer to this question, since the problem is merely shifted one stage further back, and requires first of all a decision as to what trust one should place in the eye-witness accounts as compared with the views of sceptical zoologists. The outcome of such a process of balancing the pros and cons on the part of any particular person will to a large extent depend on his pre-existing opinions and beliefs; and in this way it is largely subjective. With this kind of issue it is very rarely possible to arrive at any objective assessment of probabilities. Where such probabilities are cited, it is advisable to look closely at their basis, as the following example will illustrate. Kirwan, a geologist and president of the Royal Irish Academy at the beginning of the nineteenth century, offered proof of the creation of the earth as described by Moses. He claimed that there were 'seven or eight geological facts' related by Moses which also emerged 'from the most exact and best verified geological observations':

That two accounts derived from sources totally distinct from and independent of each other should agree not only in substance but in the order of succession of two events only, is already highly improbable, if these facts be not true, both substantially and as to the order of their succession. Let this improbability, as to the substance of the facts, be represented only by $1/10$ then the improbability of their agreement as to seven events is $1^7/10^7$, that is, as one to ten million, and would be much higher if the *order* had entered into the computation.[3]

The initial assessment of improbability is already open to question, but this is a minor point. The supposed parallelism of the story by Moses and the geological 'facts' arises from an incredibly far-fetched re-interpretation; for example the spirit of God moving on the face of the waters was taken to refer to 'the great *evaporation* that took place as soon as the solids began to crystallize'. This goes to show that with an imaginative effort a semblance of impressive probabilities can be produced, but this is little guide to truth or falsehood. Professor Heath's view that if probabilities are not calculable, the belief is a superstition, will not stand up to scrutiny either. Fresh scientific discoveries are a case in point; here probabilities are normally judged on existing knowledge, which often leads to initial rejection of a new idea. Thus when Roentgen announced his discovery of X-rays, he was widely ridiculed – such entities were too improbable to be believed by many of his scientific contemporaries. Each new discovery renders some of the old probability judgements obsolete and creates a basis for new ones.

The same line of thought leads to the conclusion that 'superstition' is a term relative to time and place. In the Middle Ages, Europe was steeped in beliefs which we would today describe as 'superstitious'. The world as people saw it included witches, devils, fairies and all kinds of strange beasts; their medicine was compounded with magic, and miracles were commonplace. In this world lived the vast bulk of the population, from humble peasant to learned scholar, sceptics being few and questioning only some of the more extravagant beliefs. Moreover, since most of these beliefs were closely interwoven with religious ones into one world-view, sceptics were in an important sense maladjusted, deviants who risked their lives if their doubts were too openly voiced.

Nowadays in the West witches and fairies are largely relegated to children's story books, devils have been almost wholly banished and weird beasts survive only on coats of arms. In other parts of the world, however, such beliefs remain very much alive, and one can in the second half of the century still listen to the confessions of witches accusing themselves of having killed people supernaturally.

It might perhaps be thought that much of this argument is little more than hair-splitting: certain beliefs are clearly and *demonstrably* false, so that we should be fully justified in calling them 'superstitions'. Unfortunately matters are not as simple as that. First of all, a negative proof is generally hard to establish. Thus the critics of experiments purporting to prove extra-sensory perception proceed by pointing out weaknesses in the experimental design that leave room for alternative interpretations of the results obtained. The most they usually succeed in doing is to throw doubt on a particular series of experiments; the believers almost invariably remain unmoved, since they assess the probabilities on a different basis; and there are new experiments coming along from time to time, each of which has to be demolished in turn – a truly Sisyphean task!

Furthermore, as has already been pointed out in discussing

the suggestion made by Heath for an objective definition of 'superstition', falsity is always relative to a given state of knowledge. Thus there has long been a belief in most societies that a pregnant woman is in a particularly vulnerable state; hence on the one hand she needs to observe certain precautions and avoidances, often explained in terms of increased danger from evil spirits and suchlike, and on the other she enjoys certain privileges such as being allowed to indulge in particular kinds of food she fancies. The kind of experience a woman has during pregnancy was thought to influence the offspring in various ways. These effects were not usually as dramatic as in the case of the lady from Guildford who in 1726 was said to have brought forth a litter of rabbits after having been frightened by one of these animals, an event attested both by the local midwife and a 'Surgeon and Anatomist to his Majesty'; but a large variety of unfortunate outcomes have been recorded as a result of unfavourable pre-natal experiences. Even during the enlightened Victorian era it was widely held that women 'in a certain condition' should take care to expose themselves only to pleasant stimulation, to visit art galleries and concerts, so that their child would be cultured as well as healthy. During the same period, many physicians contributed observations to medical journals suggesting that pre-natal influences were operating. Subsequently, for the first half of the twentieth century, all this came to be dismissed as 'superstition'. In a delightful book, to which the present writer is indebted, Bergen Evans[4] included the notion of pre-natal influences as an example of 'nonsense'. Studies carried out during the last two decades, however, support the view that not only physical illness of the mother but also the experience of psychological stress can adversely affect the foetus; this may result in malformations or defects in the nervous system, producing intellectual or behaviour disturbances. These studies arose from the observations of a general increase in malformations during the immediate post-war period in Germany. Thus a topic which, in the words of Dr Stott, who is one of the workers in this field, had 'fallen under the taboo of "old wives' tales"' received again serious scientific attention and was found to have a substantial factual core. It turns out that the recommendation to pregnant women to keep

7

cheerful in pleasant settings was really sound advice rather than 'superstition'.

This being so, would it not be a good idea to embark on systematic researches of various kinds of 'superstitions' so as to discover if they contain an element of truth? In principle this may be so, but in practice there are pitfalls in this sort of inquiry. Suppose an investigation were undertaken to verify whether Friday 13th is in truth an unlucky day. For this purpose one might compare the accident rate of those particular days with that on other days. Now let us suppose we do in fact find it to be significantly higher in a statistical sense, so that our result is unlikely to be due to mere chance: could we then conclude that the belief is true, and therefore not a 'superstition'? Many people would be reluctant to do so and, contrary to the evidence, might prefer to rely on the let-out that it was just a coincidence. However, such an easy way out overlooks the important fact that beliefs are not just things inside people's heads – they do affect behaviour; let us remember that beliefs about witchcraft led to the tragic death of numerous victims. Now if a considerable number of individuals firmly hold that Friday 13th is unlucky, this might well affect their behaviour on that particular day, make them more uncertain, jumpy and anxious; hence the heightened accident rate could actually be the outcome of the belief, and there is evidence that such causal sequences seem to operate. This kind of process has been dubbed 'the self-fulfilling prophecy', and is not uncommon in human affairs. For instance, to take an uncomfortably practical example, if foreign investors believe that the £ is going to fall, they will sell their holdings, which will cause the £ to fall. The prevalence of such processes would bedevil many attempts to test the truth or otherwise of 'superstitious' beliefs. Moreover, the evidence is all too frequently open to more than one interpretation, as may be illustrated by a recent case.[5]

An apparently healthy middle-aged woman, mother of five children, was admitted in March 1965 to a hospital in Canada for a minor operation. This was straightforward and went as expected, the woman regaining consciousness before leaving the theatre. An hour later she suddenly collapsed, and in spite of every effort by the doctors died the following morning. Post-mortem examination revealed extensive haemorrhage mainly of the adrenal glands, without any other pathology that might explain it. Later the surgeons were informed that she had been to a fortune-teller at the age of five, who had told her that she would die at the age of forty-three; her forty-third birthday was one week before the operation, and she had told her sister and one of the nurses that she did not expect to survive it.

These, leaving out medical details, are the facts: what conclusions can be drawn from them? The surgeons suggested the possibility that the prophecy indirectly caused the fatality; in their own words, 'We wonder if the severe emotional tensions of this patient superimposed on the physiological stress of surgery had any bearing upon her death'. Implicitly this admits another interpretation which will be frequently met in these pages, namely mere coincidence. Not surprisingly they fail to consider a third possibility, that the death was not only causally unrelated to the prophecy, but served to confirm the prescience of the fortune-teller; people who believe that the future can be revealed to us, on the other hand, may well seize upon this last interpretation and ignore the others.

In fact, there is some support for the surgeons' views from studies of infra-human animals. Barnett[6] studied the behaviour of rats introduced into an established colony. These were always attacked by at least one of the established residents, and although the actual injuries sustained were slight if not negligible, the newcomer frequently died. Post-mortem examination indicated that one of the organs most radically affected was the adrenal gland; it may well be, therefore, that such a response to intense stress is common to various mammals.

This has been a lengthy exploration, which has not led us any nearer to the goal of defining 'superstition'. On the contrary, it ought to be evident by now that there is no objective means of distinguishing 'superstition' from other types of belief and action. In order to escape from this impasse it will be necessary to fall back on a convenient device used by lawyers, namely the notion of the 'reasonable man'; anybody objecting to this particular fiction is of course free to substitute something like 'the consensus

9

of educated people', which will do just as well. At any rate, hereafter the word 'superstition' will be used in the sense of the kind of belief and action a reasonable man in present-day Western society would regard as being 'superstitious'. With this subterfuge the inverted commas can now be dropped.

Before leaving the subject, it ought to be made clear what this means: if a particular belief or practice is referred to as a superstition, this is merely based on the present writer's judgement that the consensus of well-informed contemporaries would regard it as such. Needless to say, such a judgement may well be wrong; and if a reader finds a cherished belief thus labelled, his mind will be set at rest by putting this down to a gross misjudgement on my part. However, the real question at issue is not whether every single example quoted is correctly classified as superstition. The aim is to examine the psychological aspects of such kinds of belief, and as long as there is reasonable agreement about the majority of the instances discussed there is no cause for any quarrel.

Having arrived at a working definition, the range of beliefs and practices covered by it remains vast: from lucky or unlucky numbers, days or colours via astrology and other occult systems to witches, ghosts and sorcerers. At the outset, therefore, some attempt will have to be made to reduce all this to some kind of order, and several major categories of superstition will be distinguished. These are fairly wide, and the boundaries between them not always clear-cut. Other classifications are possible, the reason for selecting this particular one being merely that it fits in more conveniently with the various theoretical schemes presented in subsequent chapters.

SUPERSTITION FORMING PART OF A COSMOLOGY OR COHERENT WORLD-VIEW

This is the kind closely associated with various forms of so-called 'pagan' religions. There was a time when such religions were regarded *in toto* as nothing but superstition. Today we in the West have become less confident that our own ideals and values are the only worthwhile ones, and more tolerant of those of others. Hence there is a greater appreciation of, and even respect for, the religious ideas of other cultures. It is also being recognized that, as in classical Greece, there is often a genuinely religious core shading imperceptibly into crude magical beliefs and practices at the periphery. A brief sketch of the traditional Ashanti world-view will convey some idea of such a varied spectrum.[7]

The Ashanti conceived the universe as containing a hierarchy of spirits, with a Supreme Being or Creator at the apex. This Great, Powerful and Eternal One has most of the attributes of the God of monotheistic religions. At the same time, this Great Spirit was felt as being somewhat remote, his power becoming manifest only through lesser gods, and it is these latter only which are served by priests. The most important of these deities are spirits of rivers, but others may relate to trees, animals or even charms. The minor gods are not, however, confined to these physical locations:

> The god requires a temporary abode and a priest. The temporary abode may be a tree or river, or a rock; or a priest might prepare for the spirit of his god a wooden image or mound of mud daubed with blood and placed in a basin and kept in a temple. The god will not always be present in this temporary abode which he enters at will or when called there by the priest.[8]

On the other hand, in the more narrow sense of animism, animals and trees also have souls, and when these are powerful ones they have to be propitiated. Thus the drummer on the talking drums invokes the spirit of the cedar tree from which the drum is made when he begins a ceremonial performance:

> Spirit of the Cedar tree,
> The Creator's drummer announces,
> That he has made himself to arise
> As the cock crowed at dawn.
> We are addressing you, and you will understand.[9]

The most pervasive spirits and those most intimately associated with the well-being of the living are those of ancestors, who are believed to be constantly concerned with the fate of their relatives. If people live good lives, their ancestors will help and bless them, but otherwise they may be punished. Funeral dirges dramatically express this feeling of dependence of the living on the dead:

Mother Aba, the great Breast that children suck,
Mother Aba, the great wooden Food Bowl around
    which children gather . . .
Mother, you know our plight:
Don't go too far away from us.[10]

This world-view of a hierarchy of spirits, often subtly and
poetically expressed, encompasses equally a variety of beliefs for
which the label of superstition is appropriate. Charms and talismans have already been mentioned, but the Ashanti world is
also inhabited by witches, dwarfs in the forest who are said to
have taught men both white and black magic, and lastly a horrible
hairy monster, *sasabonsam*, alleged to prey on people in the bush.
In the past European travellers visiting such places as Ashanti
would pick up weird, exotic and perhaps repellent aspects of
indigenous beliefs and practices, often to castigate the supposed
stupidity and wretchedness of people whose ways of living and
thinking they failed to understand. Today anthropologists look
at such religious and magical beliefs in the context of the culture
as a whole and, as will be indicated later, show how they fit
meaningfully into a particular pattern of social relations. The
students of society are no longer invariably outsiders; for instance
Dr Busia is himself an Ashanti.

Many of the old beliefs are of course disappearing with the
spread of Western education and technology – it is difficult now
to find people who still take *sasabonsam* seriously. What is more
surprising, and needs careful examination, is the fact that other
types of traditional belief and practice persist unabated, side by
side with Western ideas. There are university-trained Ashanti
firmly convinced of the existence of forest dwarfs and of witchcraft, and some observers have formed the opinion that among
the population at large the prevalence of such beliefs is in fact
increasing.

In general this first category of superstition associated with a
wider traditional world-view is somewhat uneasily located in
the no-man's-land separating religion from superstition. There
is thus room for argument as to what ought to be included or
omitted, and in the main our concern in this sphere will be with
magic, sorcery and witchcraft.

Some of these may in the past have been part of a broader system of ideas and beliefs, but at present they consist for the most part of isolated elements handed down by tradition, which have not yet lost their potency. A large proportion of such superstitions are concerned with good and bad luck, either as omens or practices supposedly offering protection. Examples would be breaking mirrors, spilling salt, horseshoes, wishing wells, 'touching wood', charms, talismans, and so on. Others relate to important events in the life cycle such as weddings or christenings, and many occupations have their own set of superstitions. Ill-health is surrounded with them, and folk-medicine is by no means extinct. It is as well to be cautious here, though, because some popular notions turn out to have solid factual foundations. Thus when Edward Jenner, the discoverer of vaccination, was an apprentice in his teens he heard about a local belief in Gloucestershire that people infected by cow-pox from cattle were thereafter immune from smallpox. Contemporary physicians refused to pay any attention to such tales, but these probably inspired Jenner's later experiments. He kept them secret at first, rightly suspecting that his colleagues were not inclined to take them seriously. Nonetheless, while there may be the occasional nugget among the dross, the bulk of folk-medicine probably deserves to be classed as superstition; this is not to say that it may not do some good through the *placebo* effect, whereby benefit can be derived from any remedy in which one genuinely believes. Most of these beliefs and practices have considerable antiquity; often they become adapted to modern conditions of life (mascots now appear in cars and planes) and new ones do emerge from time to time; chain letters for instance must be of fairly recent origin.

Advantage is taken of people's continued readiness to accept superstitions by practitioners like fortune-tellers, be they gipsy palmists or astrologers in pretentious offices. Here one sees a professional specialization where somewhat intangible services can be purchased from self-styled experts in the supernatural. Distinct from such occupations which trade in superstition, but partly overlapping with them, are groups of people holding beliefs in common; these may concern mediums and the spirits of the departed, flying saucers and contact with denizens of other planets, or a re-vamped version of old-fashioned witchcraft. All such may be regarded as institutionalized forms of superstition, whereby people not only hold similar beliefs but also interact socially and work together for the furtherance of goals related to these beliefs.[11]

'OCCULT' EXPERIENCES OF INDIVIDUALS

This category does beg the question to some extent, in so far as some of these experiences may be held to be genuine. The alleged phenomena are of different kinds, ranging from those on which even scientific opinion is genuinely divided to others which few educated people would care to defend. An example of the former is extra-sensory perception (ESP), regarded by some respected scholars as scientifically established beyond reasonable doubt, while others equally competent reject the evidence as untrustworthy.[12] This continued acute and often acrimonious controversy again illustrates the difficulty of arriving at any 'objective' judgements in such matters.

ESP is of course a relatively narrow and highly specialized field, involving laboratory studies and sometimes highly sophisticated gadgetry. The bulk of so-called spontaneous phenomena lies outside it, and there are innumerable reports of all kinds of paranormal experiences: visions of ghosts, haunted houses, poltergeists, forebodings of disaster and death. An impartial body concerned with such problems, the Society for Psychical Research, makes it its business to investigate many such reports that come to its notice. The overwhelming majority of such cases fail to stand up to careful scrutiny. Premonitions are usually proclaimed after the event has actually occurred, and people were therefore invited to deposit such predictions with the Society. Dr D. J. West[13] followed up thirty-two prophecies concerning mostly wars, horse-racing and deaths; of all these, not a single one had been fulfilled. It is true that in the Society's files there remains a small core of well-authenticated cases of apparently paranormal phenomena that cannot be readily dismissed.[14] It would therefore be unwise to dismiss the whole business altogether; on the other hand the large mass of such alleged experiences are clearly spurious, and this is the justification for classing them as superstitions.

It should be noted that this category overlaps in some degree with the preceding one. People who attend a seance feel that they have 'occult' experiences, but these are of course shared among the members present. Ghosts are sometimes reported as having been seen by several people in the same place, and this also applies to poltergeists. It is not possible or necessary to draw a sharp line between these categories, though the social element will have to be specially considered.

PERSONAL SUPERSTITIONS

These are beliefs and practices individuals have come to adopt by and for themselves, usually without communicating them to others. They must not be confused with socially shared superstitions applied to a particular person. For instance, in the magic of numbers there is a system whereby each letter of the alphabet has a numerical equivalent, and in applying this code one can find out one's own lucky number by successive summing of the digits, as shown below:

$$
\begin{array}{ccccc}
\text{C} & \text{O} & \text{L} & \text{I} & \text{N} \\
3 & 6 & 3 & 9 & 5 \\
& & 26 & & \\
& & \underline{8} & &
\end{array}
$$

This, however, is merely the specific application of a general principle, and as such would not be considered a personal superstition. On the other hand, if someone in time comes to think that 8 is his lucky number, without ever having come across numerology, this would be a genuine personal superstition. People may have their own private lucky or unlucky colours, days, objects or places. They may perform certain ritual acts in order to ensure success in their undertakings or ward off some danger. For instance, a friend of mine confessed that in embarking on a piece of writing he always used a particular kind of pen without which he felt he would not be able to do well. Some of these actions partake of the nature of divination ('If I manage to hit the tree three times with a stone, my wish will be fulfilled'). Again, it may be a specific sign that is looked for to determine whether or not a given outcome is likely to be propitious; I find this happening sometimes to myself, and recall an occasion when the thought obtruded itself 'if the signal light changes from red to green before disappearing from view behind the house, things will work out all right'. No doubt many readers will be able to bring to mind similar experiences.[15]

Some people are firmly convinced of the efficacy of their private rituals or oracles, although they may be reluctant to admit this to the scoffer. Others are intellectually well aware of the futility of their gestures, laugh about the whole thing, and yet persist in going through the motions. It is likely that most people are somewhere in between these two attitudes.

REFERENCES

1 W. H. Mallock, London: Ward & Downey, 1895.
2 'Probability, Science and Superstition', *The Rationalist Annual*, 1948.
3 Quoted in C. C. Gillespie, *Genesis and Geology*, New York: Harper, 1959.
4 *The Natural History of Nonsense*, Michael Joseph, 1947.
5 From a letter in the *British Medical Journal*, 7 August 1965.
6 S. A. Barnett, 'Physiological effects of "social stress" in wild rats – I. The adrenal cortex', *Journal of Psychosomatic Research*, 1958, 3, pp. 1–11.
7 Apart from direct personal sources, this account is mainly based on the following works: K. A. Busia, 'The Ashanti of the Gold Coast', in Daryll Forde (ed.), *African Worlds*, Oxford University Press, 1954; J. B. Danquah, *The Akan Doctrine of God*, London: Lutterworth, 1944; R. S. Rattray, *Religion and Art in Ashanti*, Oxford University Press, 1927.
8 Busia, *op. cit.*, p. 193.
9 *Ibid.*
10 J. H. Nketia, *Funeral Dirges of the Akan People*, Achimota, 1955, p. 10.
11 The characteristics of such groups of 'believers' of all kinds have been discussed by Hans Toch (*The Social Psychology of Social Movements*, Methuen, 1966).
12 The case for is presented by R. H. Thouless (*Experimental Psychical Research*, Penguin Books, 1963) and that against by C. E. M. Hansel (*ESP: a scientific evaluation*, New York: Scribners, 1966).
13 'The investigation of spontaneous cases', *Proceedings of the Society for Psychical Research*, 1948, 48, pp. 264–300.
14 See A. Mackenzie, *The Unexplained*, London: Barker, 1966.
15 This is discussed by Carveth Read (*The Origin of Man and of his Superstitions*, Cambridge University Press, 1920, p. 115).

The Prevalence of Superstition

In Africa, the Women's Guilds and mothers' meetings of
the churches are the embattled advance guard in a des-
perate fight against the forces of witchcraft and superstition
enslaving a continent and its people.

> From an article in a church magazine, January 1966

There is a robust nineteenth-century complacency in the above
outburst – they are superstitious and we are enlightened. How
far is either true? Let us admit, first of all, that 'they' are indeed
superstitious. This has already been indicated with reference to
traditional beliefs, and there is no doubt that notions of witchcraft, sorcery and magic remain well entrenched in Africa today.
Such notions are by no means confined to traditional spheres of
life, but have become adapted to modern Western ones. Magical
medicines are widely available for passing examinations or gaining
promotion in one's job. In Ghana in 1955 it was found necessary
to amend the electoral law so that anyone who, among other
things,

... administers, invokes or makes any other use of any fetish, or
makes any other invocation, or purports to cast any spell, and relates
any such act to or connects any such act with the voting or refraining
from voting by any person at any election shall be guilty of an offence.

Since then there have been many reports about magic becoming
mixed up with politics from other parts of Africa. But why single
out Africa? In India the astrologers have an important voice in the
land. Readings are usually taken before marriages are contracted,
and the advice of the stars is often sought for other important decisions. When the astrologers prophesied the end of the world

17

for 5 February 1962 there was general consternation, with vast sections of the population either preparing for the doom or attempting to ward it off with round-the-clock prayer sessions, fortunately successful. Indians also have a remarkable faith in the miracles of which various holy men are supposed to be capable. One of these in 1966 promised to walk on the surface of water, and a crowd of spectators paid nearly £3,000 to watch the feat. The outcome can be seen in a photograph showing the venerably bearded Hatayogi Laxman Sandra standing chest-deep in a tank of water, looking disconsolate.[1] There are many far-away places steeped in all kinds of superstition and we can have some quiet fun at their expense, or bemoan their backwardness, on the smug assumption that we have left all this behind. Is this assumption justified, and are we really as enlightened as we like to think? The answer is not easy to come by. First, because of the difficulty already discussed at length of deciding what is to be regarded as superstition and, second, because the empirical evidence is scarce. Most of the available information relates to socially shared superstitions and alleged occult experiences. In an attempt to build up some kind of a picture, two complementary modes of approach will be used: to begin with, a somewhat impressionistic and anecdotal one, followed by an account of various surveys that have been undertaken.

SOME PUBLIC MANIFESTATIONS OF SUPERSTITION

Those easiest to identify are superstitions which have an influence on overt behaviour. Among the most powerful of these is the one concerning the number thirteen. Hostesses avoid having this number of guests, and an error can lead to serious embarrassment. As it happens, I was present at a children's party on the day this is being written, where one of the mothers discovered that there were thirteen children at the table; she was seriously worried about this, insisting that another be found to ward off the danger. The importance of such fears is often publicly acknowledged, as in some American hotels which omit the unlucky floor, so that the fourteenth is above the twelfth; and when the Queen visited West Germany in 1965, the stationmaster at Duisburg arranged to change the number of the platform from which the Queen's train was due to depart from 13 to 12A. Other superstitions are equally a matter of everyday experience in our society, as for instance the touching of wood by people who say something about their good fortune; there will be occasion to examine this practice in depth in a later chapter.

It is my experience, which others have also had,[2] that when a group of people in this country are gathered together and the talk comes around to the supernatural, the chances are that several persons will tell stories of occult occurrences that allegedly happened either to themselves or their relatives and friends; such stories are apt to range all the way from vague premonitions to seeing ghosts. Most of this remains part of the vast anonymous underground of superstition which emerges only on special occasions in private conversations. A small fraction does become public under certain circumstances, for instance when it is particularly sensational, concerns prominent people or involves the religious or legal authorities. Even a mere casual scanning of the press yields a rich harvest, showing that even in the second half of the twentieth century and in Europe the supernatural is news. A selection of headlines (with brief explanatory comments added where necessary) will serve as illustration, beginning with ghosts and evil spirits.

Home to meet a ghost. Rating flown from Malta'. His wife was troubled by a black and white phantom without a head, who punched her three young children.

'Workers pray to stop a hoodoo'. Two directors and a foreman had died suddenly at work. The minister is quoted as saying, 'The men in the factory who fear a hoodoo are really tough, hardy types'.

'Men saw "ghost in crinoline" in mansion. Judge told that coats left their shoulders'.

'Strange happenings in baroness's home. Minister prays to stop ghosts'.

'A night of terror in the old theatre'. Nightwatchman sees the ghost of a young woman.

'"Evil spirits" in house. Five sleepless nights'. A coal merchant driven from his council house by strange happenings and noises.

These beliefs do receive occasional support from individuals in positions of high status and prestige:

'Haunted houses exist, says Oxford Professor. Apparitions of living and dead: crystal gazing's role'. Report of a speech.

'Canon E.B., of Oxford, said that he had a profound belief in angels and, therefore, in devils or evil spirits. He believed that many patients in our hospitals were really possessed by demons rather than suffering from diseases of the mind'. Report of a speech at the Convocation of Canterbury.

Numerous cases reach courts of law when unscrupulous people exploit the gullibility of their fellows for their own ends; many more probably occur, where those duped are reluctant to expose themselves to a public hearing. One case is cited from Moscow to indicate that such attitudes of mind are by no means absent in communist countries.

'We paid gipsy £1,400 to lift spells, say women'. The gipsy claimed to be the seventh child of a seventh child, with second sight. She promised to restore the ladies' fortunes by 'turning the planets', whatever that may mean.

The case of the 'exultation of flowers'. The accused claimed for this concoction that it cured all manners of diseases, mental as well as physical, and was a veritable elixir of youth. It was prepared by dipping 'potent' flower heads into a stream; water was then taken from the stream, which constituted the medicine in concentrated form. It was then diluted 330 times with ordinary water, and bottled. About 21,600 bottles were sold at a price of over 10s. per 2 oz. bottle.

'Marriage advice "swindle"'. A Moscow housewife ran a 'save your marriage' mail order service, promising to restore harmony. According to *Pravda* the cure consisted of taking an ordinary piece of paper, folding it, and putting it near one's bed. An alarm must be set for midnight, and when it rings one tears a strip off the paper. The operation is to be repeated if necessary, and if it still fails one can throw earth out of the window or burn a few of one's hairs.

While an unknown number of those who batten on superstition operate outside the law, others remain on the right side of it. In this age of the computer and the moon rocket, astrology and fortune-telling are enjoying a boom. Information about the number of full-time practitioners is hard to come by, since the Registrar-General classifies fortune-tellers under the broad category of 'service, sport and recreation workers'. It is estimated that there are probably some 2,000 professionals in Britain today, getting a comfortable four-figure income, apart from the 'stars' who can achieve five figures. Regular customers are supposed to number over a million. Methods vary from card or teacup reading via crystal gazing to astrology; practitioners of the latter offer their clients anything from printed slips (disapproved by 'serious' astrologers) to individually calculated horoscopes. Prominent astrologers and clairvoyants receive notice in the press, and appear on television.

Harder facts are available for publications, which have mush-roomed over the past generation. Many newspapers and magazines carry astrological columns. In the United States it was estimated that in the early sixties more than 1,000 papers had them, with some 20 million readers. In Britain there are several magazines catering for a taste in prophecy and the occult. One of these has a circulation of 50,000 copies per month, others keep theirs secret. Paperback publishers have also raised their sights to the stars, and one of them was reported to have issued a collection of astrological books with a first printing of 750,000 copies.[3]

A minor part of commercial superstition is the sale of charms, lucky mascots or talismans. As mass-produced articles these must have a wide sale, though details are not readily obtainable. There are also specialists who produce tailor-made talismans for specific purposes relating to love, health or wealth. These are manufactured by people 'skilled in the occult arts', and 'a true talisman attracts specially the vibrations of the particular planet that causes the effects you desire'; unlike the mass-produced ones, these cost from a few guineas upwards.

There also exist a variety of agencies or societies purporting to initiate those who join them, on payment of a substantial fee, into the secrets of the cosmos and the mastery of their life. In some of these the occult component is predominant, whilst others shade into devices for the improvement of memory. One very large area has barely been touched upon, and that concerns the widespread practice of unorthodox medicine. This is a controversial field and an able, in part even convincing, defence of such practices has been put forward by Brian Inglis.[4] However, after making every reasonable allowance it is likely that many of the pseudo-scientific devices like the 'black box', which seems to provide many of its operators with an opulent income, would probably deserve to come within our definition.

All this adds up to the fact that there appears to be a very substantial market for products of a somewhat indefinable nature which have value only in so far as the purchaser is open to super-stitious beliefs.

Another form of superstition that survives in Europe is the belief in sorcery and witchcraft. Cases are reported from time to time in Germany, France and, above all, southern Italy. I had occasion to discuss this with an Italian doctor, member of a health research centre, who commented after a lecture on African witchcraft that much the same beliefs and practices were prevalent in the area he was studying.[5] Nor is this absent from rural areas in Britain. A witness at an inquiry conducted by the British Medical Association reported as follows: 'The practice of magic, both black and white, was widely spread in my Devon practice. I had one definite death from witchcraft, or I suppose I should say suggestion, while I was there. The practice of charming away warts is extremely effective.'[6]

All these are perhaps best regarded as survivals, possibly moribund though by no means totally extinct. A related but in many ways very different phenomenon is the rise of organized witchcraft and the formation of twentieth-century-style covens. Members celebrate their sabbath by dancing around naked, performing various rituals, and follow this up with a picnic in the woods. The movement has attracted a certain amount of publicity, and on the occasion of the publication of a book on witches several of them were interviewed on the BBC Home Service; they did not hesitate to claim all kinds of supernormal powers. Occasionally reports also appear in the press:

An attractive, fair-haired Scots housewife admitted last night: 'I am a Witch Queen.' And her husband added: 'I also practise witchcraft. I am a high priest of our movement.' They were sitting together on a sofa in the living room of their neat bungalow ... Then they spoke for the first time about the incredible sect that they claim operates underground in Scotland today . . .

They boasted about several magical achievements, such as producing sunshine for a farmer (in Africa it is usually rain), and getting a student through his finals. The 'high priest' was said to be a former fighter pilot, now a senior executive with a firm. From many of these accounts one gets the impression that contemporary covens tend on the whole to be middle-class in their membership; incidentally, there is a curious lack of reticence to talk about activities that are supposed to be highly secret, and even photographs of witches have appeared.[7] All the same, total numbers are uncertain – 30,000 has been mentioned, but this is probably little more than a guess. At any rate, the numerical importance of the modern witchcraft cult is small, though it is remarkable that a movement with roots in the dark and remote past appears to be gaining ground. Its polar opposite is perhaps the Aetherius Society, a cult whose adherents suppose themselves to be in touch with people from outer space; some indeed claim to have made trips in flying saucers.[8] In between there flourishes a bewildering variety of cults, which have never been adequately examined. The most sizeable of these often purport to be able to communicate with the dead, largely through the intermediary of professional mediums.

Such organizations are also very common in the US. After J. B. Rhine published his first researches on ESP, he seems to have been inundated with letters from such sources, which led to the following *cri de cœur*:

In spite of years of inquiry with some phase or other of this subject I had never dreamed there were so many brands and branches of the 'occult sciences' as there really are in practice in this country. How many strange cults and odd philosophies seem to be established and flourishing, how many imposing titles that imply ascendent powers of mind and body, how many opportunities for the development of one's hidden capacities![9]

Enough has been said to indicate that under the seemingly rational surface of modern society there is an unexpectedly widespread yearning for the mysterious and occult we are supposed to have outgrown. One further concrete example may perhaps be cited. Some years ago, the extra-mural department of a university included among the list of its courses one which promised to deal with 'psychic' phenomena. Whilst many of the more conventional classes in the arts and sciences attracted barely enough people to survive, there was an overwhelming rush for this particular one; not only had other more spacious accommodation to be found, but the classes had to be laid on more than once.

It may well be objected that the preceding sketch has been selective, thereby conveying a misleading impression; the cumulative effect of listing instances of superstition may not accurately reflect the frequency with which such beliefs are actually held. There is certainly some force in this criticism, and we therefore turn to an examination of such systematic survey evidence as is available.

SYSTEMATIC SURVEYS

Superstition, being a somewhat odd and esoteric topic, has not generally been taken very seriously by students of attitude and belief, hence the evidence is somewhat scarce. On the other hand, whenever someone does take the trouble to inquire, they are often amply rewarded. Aniela Jaffé, a follower of Jung, wrote a series of articles in a Swiss newspaper dealing with such themes as prophetic dreams, ghosts and apparitions. Readers were invited to communicate with her if they had experienced anything of the kind. The response, which forms the basis of her book,[10] was remarkable: she received some 1,200 letters reporting roughly 1,500 occult experiences – this in the sober and supposedly unimaginative country of Switzerland!

The people responding to such an appeal are of course self-selected. In other words, they have an interest in occult phenomena as shown by their reading of the articles, and have as well sufficient time and energy to set down their stories. Like the people who write to the newspapers, or send protests to their MPs, they are not representative. If one wishes to get information about the extent to which various beliefs are held among the population of a country, suitable sampling methods have to be used. Fortunately there has been at least one large-scale survey in England, which among other things covered a number of superstitious beliefs and practices. There have also been several inquiries in Germany, and one very small one in Glasgow. Results are presented in detail in an appendix to this chapter, and here only the salient findings will be briefly summarized.

In England, one person in six believes in ghosts, and nearly one quarter are uncertain whether or not they exist; one person in fourteen thinks he or she has actually seen or heard a ghost. In Glasgow the proportions are substantially lower, but not negligible. In England almost one person in three has been to a fortune-teller, and some have been repeatedly – no wonder the profession is flourishing! In England at least one person in ten feels that they have lucky days or numbers, or possess lucky mascots. The percentage is much higher in Germany, and there as well as in Glasgow about half the people believe in luck. The word 'astrology' is not widely understood either in England or Germany, but practically everybody knows what a horoscope is. Everywhere about two thirds read their own horoscope at least occasionally, though serious belief in the influence of the stars ranges from roughly 1 in 3 (Germany) and 1 in 5 (England) to 1 in 10 (Glasgow), those uncertain being left out of account.

Enough has been cited to show that, apart from considerable variations to be expected from differing samples and methods, there is clearly a substantial minority of the general population in England and Germany (and probably also in other European countries) who hold decidedly superstitious beliefs. Moreover, detailed breakdowns according to social background of the informants indicate that such beliefs are by no means confined to the poor and ignorant. On this there is also some quite independent evidence concerning students in the United States and Britain, also set out more fully in the appendix. Some of the questionnaire items reproduced there may be said to relate to misinformation rather than superstition, but there appears a surprising incidence of belief in palm-reading, the influence of the stars, or dogs' ability to sense impending disaster. Here again one encounters wide variations in prevalence, no doubt due partly to differences in time, place, composition of the sample and modes of asking questions. Nonetheless, it does emerge that students are by no means exempt from all superstition.[11]

Although there is a modest amount of evidence about the prevalence of superstitious *beliefs* in Western industrial societies, hardly any systematic work has been done on superstitious *behaviour*, probably owing to the practical difficulties involved. One intrepid experimenter questioned a group of subjects about their superstitions and subsequently faced them with mirror-breaking, spilling of salt and so on to note their reactions;[12] the trouble was that the setting was too obviously contrived. Following an earlier lead by McKellar, some simple yet effective naturalistic observation was undertaken by Garwood.[13] He noted the behaviour of people when confronted by a ladder in position over a pavement. Of the 51 persons passing the spot during 15 minutes, 14 walked under the ladder and the rest stepped into the road so as to avoid it, thereby exposing themselves to danger from traffic; there was no one up the ladder during that time, so that any realistic risk was excluded. In spite of its modest scope this result is suggestive, and in line with that of a much more extensive study on water divining to be discussed later.

It is now time to return to the opening question: are we really fully enlightened, having left superstition behind? The sketch just provided, in spite of many regrettable gaps in the evidence, leaves no doubt that the answer must be 'no'. If one takes into account the fact that people are apt to be somewhat shamefaced about superstition, and liable to deny holding any such beliefs when faced with a strange interviewer, the evidence becomes even more impressive. Superstition is still very much with us, and it is even possible that some forms of it may be on the increase. Therefore it is well worth while trying to understand the nature of this complex phenomenon, which is a general human one not confined to distant peoples.

REFERENCES

1 For a more serious if somewhat disenchanted view of Indian Yoga see Arthur Koestler, *The Lotus and the Robot*, Hutchinson, 1960.
2 See for instance David Martin, 'The unknown gods of the English', *The Listener*, 12.5.66.

3 Some of this information is based on articles in *Time* Magazine, 28.12.62 and the *Observer Colour Supplement*, 13.3.66.

4 *Fringe Medicine*, Faber, 1964.

5 This theme is also very vividly presented in *Waste*, by Danilo Dolci.

6 *Divine Healing and Co-operation between Doctors and Clergy*, British Medical Association, 1956, p. 34.

7 *Weekend Telegraph*, No. 35, 21.5.65; also No. 90, 17.6.66.

8 cf. John Jackson, 'Two contemporary cults', *The Listener*, 19.5.66.

9 J. B. Rhine, *New Frontiers of the Mind*, Faber, 1938, p. 249.

10 *Geister-Erscheinungen und Vorzeichen*, Zurich: Rascher, 1958.

11 A recent book describes some of the beliefs of members of Mensa, a society composed of people with very high intelligence quotients. It seems that 22 per cent of them believe in the occult, 17 per cent in flying saucers, palmistry and phrenology. See V. Serebriakoff, *A Mensa Analysis and History*, Hutchinson, 1966.

12 R. Zapf, 'Comparison of responses to superstitions on a written test and in actual situations', *Journal of Educational Research*, 1945, 39, pp. 13–24.

13 'Superstition and half-belief', *New Society*, 31.1.63.

SURVEY RESULTS ON
SUPERSTITIOUS BELIEFS AND PRACTICES

These are offered in the following tables, preceded by notes on sources. In order to simplify the presentation of comparative materials, closely similar questions in different surveys have been combined into a single one.

Table 1 : Surveys of the general population

Notes

England. This is based on a large-scale survey by Geoffrey Gorer (*Exploring English Character*, Cresset Press, 1955). He invited readers of the *People* to answer a lengthy questionnaire that included material on superstition. Over 14,000 were returned and of these about a third, selected to represent the population optimally, were analysed. In addition, a field survey was organized, asking the same types of questions to provide an independent check on the validity of the questionnaire. This sample (presumably a quota one) consisted of 1,760 individuals.

Germany. The data here are drawn from an inquiry concerned primarily with belief in astrology. The information is based on a series of surveys carried out during the 1950s by the German Institute of Public Opinion on a representative sample of the population. The material was published by Gerhard Schmidtchen ('Soziologisches über die Astrologie', *Zeitschrift für Parapsychologie und Grenzgebiete der Psychologie*, 1957, 1, pp. 47–72).

Glasgow. A small inquiry was undertaken in a Glasgow parliamentary constituency, consisting mainly of a working-class population, using a random sample. The main purpose of the survey concerned some educational problems, but it was possible to include a few questions dealing with superstition.

N.B. The abbreviation 'N' refers to the number in the sample, 'N.A.' means 'no answer' and 'D.K.' means 'don't know'; in the case of England, 'Q' denotes questionnaire results and 'F' those derived from the field survey.

GHOSTS

England : Do you believe in ghosts?

   Q. (N=4,983)   Yes 17% No 58% Uncertain 23% N.A. 2%

If you believe in ghosts, have you ever seen a ghost?

   Q. (N=841)   Yes 42% No 22% Uncertain 35% N.A. 1%

Glasgow : Do you believe in ghosts, or things like that? If yes, have you ever seen a ghost?

(N=265)	Believe	Seen ghosts 1% }	7%
		Not seen 6% }	
	Don't believe		91%
	D.K.		2%

FORTUNE-TELLING

England : Have you ever been to a fortune-teller?

   Q. (N=4,983)   Yes 44%   No 53%   N.A. 3%

   F. (N=1,780)   Yes 28%   No 71%   N.A. 1%

If yes, how often have you been?

   Q. (N=2,179)   Once 45% Twice 24% Several times 31%
                      N.A. —

   F. (N=491)   Once 51% Twice 21% Several times 25%
                      N.A. 3%

Did any of it come true?

   Q. (N=2,179)   Yes 30%   Yes all 2% Yes some 15%
                   No nothing 35% D.K. 11% N.A. 7%

   F. (N=491)   Yes 29%   Yes all 3% Yes some 14%
                   No nothing 43% D.K. 11% N.A. —

LUCK

England : Have you a specially lucky or unlucky day?

   Q. (N=4,983) Lucky 9% Unlucky 5% Both 3% Neither 83%

   F. (N=1,760) Lucky: Yes 9%   No 90% N.A. 1%
                 Unlucky: Yes 7%   No 91% N.A. 2%

England : Have you a specially lucky or unlucky number?

   Q. (N=4,983) Lucky number 18% Unlucky number 3%
                 Both 3%   Neither 76%

England : Have you a lucky mascot?

   Q. (N=4,983) Yes 15%   No 82%   N.A. 3%

   F. (N=1,760) Yes 12%   No 87%   N.A. 1%

Germany : Do you find that you have in your life runs of good and bad luck, or have you not noticed anything like that?

(N=1,000)	Runs of good and bad luck	54%
	Not noticed	27%
	Cannot say	19%

Germany : Even if you yourself are not superstitious, what numbers, signs or other things predict good or bad fortune for you?

(N=1,802)	Concrete indications	46%
	Nothing predicts	50%
	No indications	4%

Glasgow : Do you believe in luck? If yes, were you yourself born lucky?

(N=265)	Yes, believe	Born lucky	23%
		Not born lucky	20%	45%
		D.K.	2%
	No, do not believe		52%
	D.K.		3%

ASTROLOGY

England : Do you read 'Lyndoe' in the *People?*

| Q. (N=4,983) | Regularly 50% | Occasionally 39% |
| | Never 10% | N.A. 1% |

Do you read the horoscope in any other paper or magazine?

Q. (N=4,983)	Regularly 35%	Occasionally 45%
	Never 17%	N.A. 3%
F. (N=1,760)	Regularly 42%	Occasionally 29%
	Never 29%	N.A. —

Do you follow the advice in the horoscope columns you read?

Q. (N=4,983)	Regularly 3%	Occasionally 22%
	Never 70%	N.A. 5%
F. (N=1,249: only regular or occasional readers)		
	Regularly 5%	Occasionally 18%
	Never 76%	N.A. 1%

Do you think there is something in horoscopes?

| Q. (N=4,983) | Yes 20% | No 44% | Uncertain 33% | N.A. 3% |
| F. (N=1,760) | Yes 17% | No 60% | Uncertain 15% | N.A. 8% |

Germany : Do you believe in a connexion between human fate and the stars?

(N=2,052)   Yes 29%   No 58%   Undecided 13%

Do you happen to have read during the past few months your daily or weekly horoscope in a newspaper or magazine?

(N=2,137) Yes, frequently 34% Yes, occasionally 27% No 39%

Do you happen to know if your horoscope at present is favourable or unfavourable?

(N=1,000)   Know the answer 25% Don't know just now 34%
             Never bother about horoscopes 41%

Glasgow : Do you believe the stars influence our life?

(N=265)   Yes 10%   No 86%   D.K. 4%

Do you read the horoscopes in newspapers and magazines?

Yes, regularly 34%   Yes, sometimes 38%   No, never 28%

Table 2 : Surveys of students

Notes

US I. This was a study carried out in the 1920s at Columbia University with classes of adult students beginning to study psychology, nearly half of whom were women. (H. K. Nixon, 'Popular answers to some psychological questions', *American Journal of Psychology*, 1925, 36, pp. 418–23).

US II. Done in 1944 with a group of pre-medical students in a state college in the United States. (L. R. Ralya, 'Some surprising beliefs concerning human nature among pre-medical psychology students', *British Journal of Educational Psychology*, 1945, 15, pp. 70–75.)

US III. A replication of US I. in 1950, also at Columbia with a similar population, but confined to men. (E. E. Levitt, 'Superstitions: twenty-five years ago and today', *American Journal of Psychology*, 1952, 65, pp. 443–9.)

M. A replication of US II. with students at Manchester University. (F. W. Warburton, 'Beliefs concerning human nature in a university department of education', *British Journal of Educational Psychology*, 1956, 26, pp. 156–62.)

G. An unpublished study carried out in 1965 of the beliefs of students in a first-year undergraduate class in psychology at Strathclyde University, Glasgow.

Percentages of Superstitious Responses in Student Samples

	US I (N = 403)	US II (N = 110)	US III (N = 141)	M (N = 143)	G (N = 121)
People born under the influence of certain planets show the influence in their character.	15	6			
The position of the stars at the time of a man's birth determines, in part, his character.			18	6	
Certain lines on a person's hand are indicative of (foretell) his future.	8	2	20	6	
Beginning an undertaking on Friday is sure to bring bad luck.	1	1	1	1	
You can make a person turn around if you stare long enough at his back.	36	10			32
A dog can sense impending disaster better than a man.					51
It is unlucky to have anything to do with the number 13.	40	3	1	1	
An English-speaking person with German blood will find it easier to learn the German language than an English-speaking person with French blood.			34	38	
Voodooism is in the blood of the Negro.			36	51	21
People with long fingers are likely to be artistic.			47	29	
Red-headed people are likely to be temperamental.	42	6	40	23	36
A large mouth is a sign of generosity.			28	16	4
A man's character can be read by noting the sizes and locations of certain developments on his head.	40	3	18	15	

CHAPTER THREE

Superstition as Error

It is in fact a sincere but fallacious system of philosophy,
evolved by the human intellect by processes still in great
measure intelligible to our own minds, and it has thus an
original standing-ground in the world. And though the
evidence of fact was dead against it, it was but lately and
gradually that this evidence was brought fatally to bear.

Tylor *The Origins of Culture*

It has just been shown that one cannot divide the peoples of the
world into the superstitious and the enlightened, but only into
those by and large more or less superstitious. A backward glance
into history teaches us the same lesson. The dominant intellectual
temper of nineteenth-century Europe was rationalistic. It is
epitomized in Comte's and Mill's serene confidence in the capacity
of the human mind to bring about orderly progress, as well as in
Darwin's shattering demonstration that the human species fits
harmoniously into a vast order of nature. However, it must not be
forgotten that there was another side; the same period saw the
spectacular rise of occultism, by no means confined to the vulgar
and ignorant. Alfred Russel Wallace, who independently hit upon
the concept of natural selection, was also an ardent believer in the
'miracles' performed by mediums, and wrote a book on the subject. His interest was first aroused when he witnessed some lec-
tures on mesmerism and phrenology by a certain Mr Hall, who
purported to prove the correctness of the relationship between
'bumps' on the skull and character with hypnotized subjects.
Wallace was severely taken to task for his gullibility by Frederic
Engels, who also saw these performances and decided to conduct
his own experiments. Engels, together with a friend, hypnotized

a young boy and in describing the results pokes a good deal of fun at Wallace:

> To put Gall's cranial organs into operation was a mere trifle for us; we went much further, we could not only exchange them for one another, or make their seat anywhere in the whole body, but we also fabricated any amount of other organs, organs of singing, whistling, piping, dancing, boxing, sewing, cobbling, tobacco-smoking etc. and we could make make their seat wherever we wanted. Wallace made his patients drunk on water, but we discovered in the great toe an organ of drunkenness which only had to be touched in order to cause the finest drunken comedy to be enacted.[1]

Wallace was not the only eminent scientist to dabble in spiritualism; for instance William Crookes, discoverer of thallium, was equally convinced of the truth of such phenomena. There were of course many others who shared the evaluation of Huxley, couched in characteristically caustic terms: 'The only good that I can see in the demonstration of the truth of 'spiritualism' is to furnish an additional argument against suicide. Better live a crossing-sweeper than die and be made to talk twaddle by a "medium" hired at a guinea a seance!' It is unlikely that the distinguished scholars who managed to reconcile science and occultism regarded themselves as being in the same class as medieval believers in witches, or 'savage' believers in shamans' spirits or medicine men's magic. Yet this is precisely how the great ethnographer Sir Edward Tylor viewed them. He suggested that a North American Indian looking on at a spirit seance in London would feel entirely at home with all the spirit manifestations such as raps, noises and voices. How can one explain such survivals? Tylor discusses this problem at length, and makes many penetrating observations. Nonetheless, the question he is actually trying to answer is 'how can error persist?'; for, as is implicit in the quotation at the head of this chapter, fundamentally he regarded superstition as an intellectual defect. When he comes to the psychological reasons, he adduces 'stupidity and unpractical conservatism' as typical of man in general and the 'savage' in particular.

The other famous ethnographer of the period, Sir James Frazer, proceeded on a somewhat similar assumption. He ob-

34

served, first, that the 'savage' fails to make a proper distinction between natural and supernatural; everything in his cosmos is personalized, and this leads him to mistaken notions about the way in which he can influence his environment. Secondly, the 'savage' has a crude philosophy based on two false principles: that like produces like, and that things which have once been in contact continue to influence each other. In *The Golden Bough* Frazer cites a mass of instances illustrating these principles, of which two may be mentioned. An example of the former, imitative magic, is the attempt to destroy an enemy by destroying his image; of the latter, contagious magic, is the practice of getting hold of some former bodily part of another person such as hair or nail parings in order to gain power over him.

Frazer claimed that such sympathetic magic plays a large part in most kinds of superstition. He viewed it as a precursor of science, an early attempt to formulate laws governing phenomena, only the laws happen to be the wrong ones. Frazer linked this misconception, as he regarded it, to the so-called 'laws of association' as formulated by John Stuart Mill, which were the king-pin of psychology until the latter part of the nineteenth century:

If we analyse the various cases of sympathetic magic which have been passed in review in the preceding pages ... we shall find them all to be mistaken applications of one or other of two great fundamental laws of thought, namely, the association of ideas by similarity and the association of ideas by contiguity in space or time. A mistaken association of similar ideas produces imitative or mimetic magic; a mistaken association of contiguous ideas produces sympathetic magic in the narrower sense of the word. The principles of association are excellent in themselves, and indeed absolutely essential to the working of the human mind. Legitimately applied they yield science; illegitimately applied they yield magic, the bastard sister of science.

Unfortunately this will not do, at any rate as it stands. Frazer wrote almost as if magicians had discovered the 'laws' of association, and had merely been guilty of stretching them unduly. It is doubtful whether he could really have meant that; more likely his notion was that the magical practices took on particular forms governed by the mode of functioning characteristic of the human

35

mind. However, stated in this manner the proposition ceases to appear illuminating and becomes trite. This is precisely the weakness of association psychology, which is essentially speculative; impressive as a system, it fails when an attempt is made to use it for the purpose of explaining particular phenomena. For this reason it was already well on the way out by the time Frazer was writing, its place being taken by more empirical approaches. One of the pioneers of this new thinking was the German psychologist Wilhelm Wundt, who in 1879 established the first psychological laboratory. Rather late in life he himself published a monumental work entitled *Völkerpsychologie*, translated somewhat quaintly as 'folk psychology'. This prolix opus, drawing heavily on Frazer, is totally divorced from Wundt's experimental studies; now deservedly forgotten, it is mentioned here only because Wundt cavalierly puts forward an interpretation of magic directly opposite to that of Frazer:

Causality, in our sense of the word, does not exist for primitive man. If we would speak of causality at all on his level of experience, we may say only that he is governed by the causality of magic. This, however, receives its stamp *not from the laws that regulate the connexion of ideas* [italics added], but from the forces of emotion. The mythological causality of emotional magic is no less spasmodic and irregular than the logical causality arising out of the orderly sequence of perceptions and ideas is constant.[2]

Calling something 'emotional' does not help us to understand it, and Wundt in this passage does little more than clothe laymen's notions in a scholarly garb. His real contribution lay in the field of experimental psychology, and he attracted a group of gifted students to his laboratory, many of whom left their mark on the emerging science. Among this group was the son of a Danish officer, Alfred Lehmann, who later occupied the chair of psychology at Copenhagen.

Lehmann's numerous writings include works on psychophysics, physiological psychology and hypnotic states. However, he was also among the few psychologists intensely interested in superstition and magic, publishing a volume with the title *Superstition and Magic*.[3] Over half the book is devoted to a mainly historical account of magical and superstitious beliefs, but the aim of the last part is to offer a psychological analysis of what Lehmann called the 'magical states of mind'.

The objective Lehmann set himself was two-fold: to show the factors which initially produce superstition, and also those responsible for its continuation. He had no illusions about the difficulty of these tasks, especially that of accounting for origins buried in the mists of time, for which, he realized, one has to rely largely on inference from known psychological principles. The ones he started with, and to which he attached considerable weight, were errors of observation and memory, and it is this aspect that will claim most of our attention. At the time, considerable progress had already been made in the study of these processes; Lehmann outlined the findings, stressing the fallibility of human senses under various conditions, and he clearly had very much in mind the conditions in which spiritualist seances were held. The experiments he conducted, which are described, all dealt with this problem. For instance, seances are usually held in dim light, which obviously makes observation difficult. However, some mediums were prepared to have a fairly bright red light, which gives the impression that the room is quite well illuminated. In order to test this, Lehmann prepared a blackboard with writing on it, which he placed at various distances from either a white or a red light. The mean distances at which it was just possible to read the lettering correctly are set out below:

	Distance of lamp from blackboard			
Maximum distance at which blackboard was able to be read in	1m	2m	4m	6m
White light	4·5m	4m	3·5m	3m
Red Light	1·5m	1m	0·5m	—

Clearly, in spite of its bright appearance, red light greatly reduces the possibility of accurate observations.

Even with optimal illumination a complex series of events is not easy to follow in detail, and further distortions are introduced in subsequent attempts to describe it. Lehmann ran a series of experiments on this theme, involving a number of magical tricks which he felt obliged to call 'psychic phenomena' in order to capture the interest of his subjects. These were friends and acquaintances, including scholars, businessmen and journalists. One of the tricks consisted of producing a piece of writing ('There are more things in heaven and earth . . .') between two small blackboards, and Lehmann quotes some of the widely divergent accounts of what had happened, none of which was really accurate; thus most subjects reported that both blackboards had been previously examined and found to be ordinary, when in fact only one had been handed out. Another particularly striking demonstration was the following: subjects were asked to select a line in a book unknown to Lehmann, who had arranged to have an unintelligible scribble appear on the blackboard. When this was suddenly presented, some of the subjects were astonished to 'read' what they thought was the correct answer, and accordingly the marvel duly appeared in their report.

When it comes to demonstrating how these various sources of error lead to superstition, Lehmann suggests two ways, a direct and an indirect one. Examples of the former would be the belief in mythical animals like the unicorn, giant snakes as described by Pliny, or more recently the sea-monk. In these cases a superstition is, as it were, said to have been newly created as a result of errors of observation and subsequent transmission of these mistaken notions. The second, indirect, aspect is that where some kind of bias enters into the observations themselves and distorts them ('*befangene Beobachtungen*'). Lehmann illustrates this from reports of comets, which were long regarded as portents; given a disposition to regard them as miraculous, it is not surprising that people imagined they saw the most extraordinary things in them such as burning beams, flaming swords, severed heads, dragons and other monsters. All these were taken to be evil omens, and there are reports of numerous misfortunes following the appearance of comets. In this connexion Lehmann rightly pointed out that the persistence of such beliefs was at least in part a function of errors of memory – what we now call selective forgetting': events that conform with predictions are singled out and cited as confirmation, whilst others that do not are glossed over and forgotten.

In addition to perception and memory, Lehmann also considered a variety of other psychological aspects of superstition. He stressed particular dreams, where he took up a position similar to that of Tylor in proposing that this was the origin of belief in ghosts; he further discussed the role of drugs in producing experiences favourable to the genesis of superstitions. Lehmann's arguments are as a rule solidly anchored in such empirical knowledge as was available at the time; he himself carried out a number of experimental studies on problems relevant to superstitious beliefs, for instance on involuntary movements involved in traditional divination, the divining rod or the ouija board. He was particularly well versed in the great controversy over spiritualism, then at its peak, and offered many a penetrating analysis of the deceptions which had fooled several eminent contemporary scientists. Nonetheless, Lehmann's basic position was that superstition is a form of error. This is clearly expressed in his summing up (p. 725): 'All the superstitious beliefs, whose natural context [*Zusammenhang*] we tried to demonstrate here, were at the beginning only false interpretations of phenomena more or less inadequately observed.'

Is this a sufficient explanation of superstition? For a variety of reasons, the answer must be 'no'. First of all, as has been shown in some detail earlier, it is by no means easy to prove that every superstition is an error. Let us take the case of the 'exultation of flowers' (see page 20 above), where the public analyst proved that the alleged medicine was in fact nothing but H_2O; the purveyor of this remedy was by no means dismayed, claiming that the effective agent was the spiritual essence, incapable of being detected by ordinary chemical analysis; and several witnesses were produced by the defence who testified that they had been cured.

It also happens that people, when challenged, will readily acknowledge that a particular action of theirs (such as 'touching wood') is a superstition without any rational basis, yet they will continue to perform it. This indicates another objection, namely that a large proportion of superstitions are not of the individual kind, but are socially transmitted. They are accepted readymade, without any intervening observations subject to error; and this aspect must also be accounted for.

39

It is not surprising, therefore, that the examples given by Lehmann were almost exclusively of two main types: spiritualist seances, where faulty observation and inference led, in his view, to a failure to detect the deceptions practised; and ancient notions about mythical animals such as the unicorn or the giant sea serpent. With regard to the latter category, anyone visiting a museum of natural history will encounter utterly grotesque specimens; mythical animals as such are perhaps not very good examples of superstition, and certainly represent only a tiny part of a very large field.

In spite of the many objections that can be raised against the view of superstition as error, it continues to be widely held:

If we inquire why so much erroneous or even absurd beliefs are held in magic and religion, one answer is that heredity, while it gives the human species superior brain capacity, does not provide a perfect thinking machine. Mistakes readily arise, which require centuries of painstaking scientific inquiry for their elimination.[4]

The rejection of error as *the* central element in superstition does of course not mean a denial that various forms of error play an important part in both the genesis and persistence of many types of superstition. A great deal more is known today than in Lehmann's time about the nature of the psychological processes involved, and in reviewing these it is hoped that not only can more light be thrown on some of the aspects dealt with by Lehmann, but that additional explanatory principles can be brought to bear on some of the phenomena.

If someone says 'I have seen it with my own eyes' or 'I heard it myself' this is apt to be regarded as conclusive evidence. While the conclusion may be reasonably justified as far as familiar everyday occurrences are concerned, it is demonstrably untenable for unusual events. In courts of law the contradictions among eye-witnesses of, say, a motor accident are notorious. In psychology courses one experiment often carried out in the past but no longer regarded as necessary was the staging of a dramatic event in the course of a lecture, such as the sudden irruption into the classroom of a man who threatened the lecturer with a pistol. Students were then asked immediately after the event to record what they had just seen, and their accounts usually diverged widely. How can such discrepancies arise?

One can turn this question around and ask: why is it taken for granted that everybody sees exactly the same thing? The answer to this is that the visual and auditory systems are, by so-called common sense, regarded as analogous to a passive recording system such as a camera or tape-recorder. In fact, the analogy is misleading in at least two different ways. First of all, an enormous amount of information reaches our sense organs all the time we are in a waking state, and a considerable amount of *selection* takes place; otherwise we would be overwhelmed. Precisely how this happens is still not entirely clear, but that it does may be exemplified by the famous 'cocktail party' problem:[5] from the buzz of conversation surrounding us we filter out one particular exchange, whilst the rest merges into diffuse background noise; other people do the same, but with a different conversation!

The second, equally important aspect is that we are frequently exposed to fragmentary and incomplete information from the outside world: somebody whispers faintly, or an object is vaguely seen in the distance. In such cases we may suspend judgement until further information becomes available, but this is not always possible – the whisper may be an urgent warning, the object a potential enemy. Then we have to make the best guess we can, based on our past experience. Although this is fairly obvious, it is less so that much of our ordinary perception is basically similar in nature; the information is commonly incomplete, and we (or rather our brains) fill in the gaps without being aware of the fact. This can be shown by presenting two different pictures separately to each eye; under certain conditions one then sees only one coherent picture, in which elements of both are combined or one of them is completely suppressed. Perception thus involves active construction on our part, not merely passive reception. In this construction, part of the materials consist of stimuli impinging from the outside, and part is drawn from our store of past experience. This experience, in turn, consists on the one hand of our own previous first-hand sense impressions, and on the other of information conveyed to us by other people. Such information may relate not only to 'real' things, but also to the objects of beliefs such as witches, spirits or giants. Where such beliefs are prevalent, external stimuli may be interpreted in terms of such alleged agencies. Thus Hallowell[6] describes an Ojibwa Indian's report of an encounter with a *Windigo*, according to this culture a cannibal giant. The Indian relates how the monster pursued him for a whole day. Close analysis by Hallowell reveals that, although the man was utterly convinced of its presence, the sensory evidence consisted exclusively of sounds. Nearer home, I have been given a first-hand account of the appearance of a ghost, where the actual sensory evidence was confined to a feeling of a chill blast of air in a room, and a dog retiring howling into a corner. These examples, which could be multiplied, should be enough to indicate ways in which the functioning of the perceptual process leaves more loop-holes than so-called 'common sense' might suggest.

It is probably less necessary to emphasize that memory is fallible. Nonetheless, it is worth pointing out that the usual notion of memory as 'footprints on the sands of time', gradually blurred and eventually erased by the wind and weather of life, is also greatly misleading. In a series of studies which have become a classic Sir Frederic Bartlett[7] has shown that the changes undergone by memory are far from being either uniform or haphazard. One of Bartlett's studies is particularly relevant, since the material to be remembered was a North American folk-tale with strong supernatural overtones. Subjects were asked to recall this story, which was a strange one for them, on several different occasions. Some of the changes that took place are in accordance with the 'common sense' view, e.g. omission of detail and simplification; others involved elaboration and invention. Most important of all, from our present standpoint, is the process Bartlett called 'rationalization'. This involves changes whereby items that were originally odd and puzzling, or inconsistent with the remainder, came to be transformed in the direction of greater unity and coherence. Moreover, the nature of such changes was in accordance with the background and dominant interests of the person recalling the story. Similar alterations take place when information is transmitted from one person to another, as has been shown by numerous experiments on rumour.

Except by experiment, it is difficult to show how these processes operate, since as a rule no independent information is available against which the remembered accounts can be checked. One famous case is quoted by West[8] from the files of the Society for Psychical Research:

Sir Edmund Horney, Chief Judge of the Supreme Consular Court in the Far East, told the story of a reporter who visited him in the middle of the night to collect a judgment handed down the previous day. Although displeased by the disturbance, Sir Edmund gave way to the pressing insistence of the man in order to avoid a scene that might have disturbed his wife. Nonetheless Lady Hornby woke up, and her husband explained what had occurred. In the morning Sir Edmund received the news that the reporter had died during the night.

This is the version, similar to many such accounts, that was published in the *Proceedings of the Society for Psychical Research*. The report reached a Mr Balfour in China, who wrote to point out that (a) there were no judgements made on the day prior to the reporter's death and (b) that Sir Edmund married three months after that event. Being unable to refute this, the judge had to concede that his memory must have grossly deceived him. There is also indirect evidence that the modifications in recall affect these stories more powerfully with the passage of time: thus in a census of hallucinations undertaken by the Society, it was observed that the most dramatic cases tended to be those alleged to have happened a long time ago.

Another way in which the distortions occurring over time can be revealed is by questioning people who have witnessed a striking performance by a conjurer or illusionist. If one knows how the trick is performed, this provides an objective base line against which the reports may be compared. I have done this with people who attended a show where a lady was being sawn in half. The reports of most of them were such that, had things really happened in the manner they described, the performer must have committed nightly homicide in public. It may be objected here that this is a case of suggestion rather than memory, and it has to be admitted that in part at least the skill of the performer consists in impression-management, whereby the attention

43

of the audience is directed towards certain aspects of the objects and events rather than others. For instance, a magician takes advantage of the fact that people will in general follow the direction of his gaze, so that if he intently fixes this on one of his hands, the chances are that an inconspicuous movement by the other will remain unobserved. Nonetheless, it can be shown that the greater the time lapse between observation and report, the more drastic are the deviations from what actually took place.

Perhaps something ought to be said about suggestion at this point, since this is a popular catchword, used in trying to explain allegedly supernatural occurrences. In the past, psychologists themselves were fond of this word; today it hardly ever figures in textbooks on the subject, for it has come to be recognized that to call anything the result of 'suggestion' is merely to attach a name to it without materially advancing our understanding. There is no single psychological process that corresponds to this term, which covers a variety of distinct phenomena. In general, suggestion refers to the exertion of an influence on another person so that he will be led towards a certain idea, belief or action. As soon as the term is spelled out in this manner, it becomes evident that this can occur in a wide variety of ways. The most direct and immediate one is hypnotic suggestion, whereby an individual becomes extremely susceptible to verbal instructions from another; a similar effect can be achieved by certain drugs, or arises during the trance state entered in the course of ritual dances.

At the opposite end of the continuum are rather subtle influences created by manipulating the expectations of a person, thereby affecting the way in which he will interpret happenings in his environment. This is linked with what has been said earlier about perceiving: by suitable 'programming' a person is provided with a particular context which will lead to one kind of construction on the basis of incoming information rather than another. This will become clearer from an example. Take a number of simple experiences: a window blind waving; pencil scribblings on a wall; an old coat hanging behind a door. Apparently nothing could be more commonplace, yet all these have been claimed as evidence for 'paranormal' phenomena in 'The Most Haunted House in England'. The writings on this by Mr Harry Price created an enormous stir at the time, and the whole issue was subjected to critical scrutiny by three investigators from the Society for Psychical Research.[9]

Price rented this rambling old house and advertised in *The Times* for observers to study the phenomena. At the outset the volunteers were given a document relating details of the alleged hauntings over a period of forty years, and instructing them on a long list of things for which they should be on the lookout; these included bell-ringing, movement of objects, footsteps, apparitions, raps and knocks, perfume, lights, apports (i.e. objects appearing), disappearances and changes of temperature. All this was under the imprint of the Honorary Secretary of the University of London Council for Psychical Investigation; although his name did not feature, this was none other than Price himself.

The advertisement recruited forty-eight observers who had to be 'intrepid', though skill in conducting this kind of investigation was not stipulated. Nonetheless, many of the observers were intelligent and highly educated people whose integrity cannot be doubted. Apart from a small sceptical minority, they reported numerous phenomena of the kind foreshadowed in their preliminary instructions. A majority were auditory – taps, cracks and thumps in the main, but also footsteps; a window blind was moving, and the observers decided there was not sufficient wind to cause it, hence it must be paranormal; an old coat hanging behind a door, which had not been previously noticed, was believed to have materialized; and while the otherwise unoccupied house was being visited by parties of observers, pencil-markings kept appearing on the walls. Such a bald listing of some of the salient phenomena reported makes them appear singularly unspectacular, perhaps almost trivial. This is actually not unusual in such cases: the stir they create rests not on the physical events as such, but on the context in which they occur and the manner in which they are interpreted. Certainly as embellished by Price the haunting of Borley Rectory became a *cause célèbre*, creating an enormous ballyhoo that went on for years. There were articles on it in the press, and the BBC ran several broadcasts on it between 1935 and 1947; two eminent lawyers publicly declared their conviction that the manifestations were genuine, one of them going so far as to say that they 'are proved by the evidence, to the point of moral certainty'.

Here we are not concerned with these wider ramifications, but merely with the reactions of the observers. The first thing to note is that they were a self-selected group of people, presumably on the whole predisposed to believe in the possibility of haunting. The instructions provided by Price served to establish not only a general expectation that paranormally caused events would occur, but also produced a mental set which increased the probability that observers would perceive and interpret particular aspects of their environment in a manner congruent with the general expectation. Such processes have been extensively studied in laboratory experiments; for instance, if subjects have been led to expect that words exposed briefly have to do with birds, the nonsense word 'pasrot' is most likely to be seen as 'parrot'; if the preceding instructions mentioned travel, the word is usually read as 'passport'. Thus the perceptions of some of the observers in the haunted house were probably subtly distorted in the direction laid down by Price. Even more important than this specific influence on perception is the wider tendency to relate every experience to the dominant theme of the supernatural, which can be seen in its most acute form in the mentally ill. Consider, for instance, the case of the man who was obsessed with the idea of his wife's unfaithfulness:

Has she a tired look? – it is proof of adultery; a gay manner – she comes from a rendezvous. A look, a movement of the eyebrows, lips or fingers are so many telltale signs; the same with smiles or tears. Should she utter the name of the supposed lover, the sound of her voice leaves no doubt; should she repeat it often, it is 'to accustom herself to hear it in public without blushing'; if she ceases to mention him, the motive can be guessed . . . His wife's footsteps on the parquet floor are so many signals to her lover and compose a telegraphic alphabet that he can successfully interpret . . .[10]

Without of course any suggestion that the observers were suffering from mental abnormality, their state was similar in so far as they felt a powerful conviction that Borley Rectory was a place where strange things occurred. Hence, quite apart from the degree of accuracy of their perceptions, many of their experiences, however commonplace they might seem to the outsider, tended to be fitted into the overall pattern of this central idea. Viewed from this perspective, the seemingly unbounded gullibility of some of the observers becomes more understandable. The aura of mystery surrounding the rectory persisted long after the building itself was destroyed by fire. One of the many people who explored its ruins lost a pencil in the area, which he was unable to recover after a prolonged search; thereupon he wrote to Price giving a detailed description of the pencil 'in case it is involved in any phenomena'.

So far the problem has been considered exclusively in terms of the psychological processes of individual persons. This was an approach characteristic of Lehmann and his time; what has been considered are the advances in this sphere since then which have a bearing upon the issue. However, beliefs and practices are rarely confined to the individual in isolation – they are usually shared with others. Some of the wider social influences will be considered in a later chapter. Here we are concerned with the results of interaction, direct and indirect, among people; on this topic a great deal has been learnt during the past quarter century which was not available to Lehmann.

Here again, we can start by examining further the alleged haunting of Borley Rectory. The instructions given to the observers, it will be recalled, were issued under the heading of a body whose title referred to the University of London, an eminently respectable institution. This will have had the effect of enhancing the confidence of the people perusing them in the authenticity of the extraordinary phenomena said to have occurred at the rectory. This used to be called 'prestige suggestion', and numerous experiments have demonstrated its power. For instance, if people are given extracts of the writings by the same obscure author, some under a well-known literary name and others under an unknown one, they will tend to judge the passages attributed to the famous figure as being far better than the others. There is a somewhat mysterious flavour about the former term 'prestige suggestion', which is easily dispelled. The underlying principle, which has been elaborated systematically by Festinger,[11] is simply that where objective, non-social means cannot be used, people assess their opinions and judgements by comparison with the opinions and judgements of others. Thus, in the example cited, those (and they are a majority) who do not feel confident of their capacity for critically evaluating a piece of writing use as their guide the name of the author, knowing that others more competent than they are have agreed that he is a great writer. There is nothing absurd or shameful about this; most of us, most of the time, are not in a position to verify the vast majority of the opinions or even 'facts' to which we subscribe *except* by reference to the statements of others whom we trust as being authoritative.

A framework was thus provided wherein the observers could order their perceptions, which many of them duly did. One detailed example will indicate the way in which mysteries arose. Two observers were standing on a landing outside a room on a September evening. They heard a rustling noise below and went down the stairs, where they discovered that a sack of coal had been moved about eighteen inches; they reported this phenomenon to Price, who included it in his book. Let us now look at this event from the standpoint of the investigators, who analysed it critically, asking a number of pertinent questions. How did the rustling noise come to be attributed to the alleged movement of the sack? In an old house a large variety of different causes (creepers rubbing against the outside wall, papers being blown about, activities of mice) could result in such noises. How did the observers know that the sack had been moved from its original position? It was stated that one of the observers had noted a stain close to the sack earlier in the day; however, no attempt had been made to mark its position deliberately, and it seems unlikely that any particular importance had been attached to the position of the sack prior to the alleged movement.

Going beyond the cautious comments of the SPR investigators, it is possible to speculate about what might have been the actual sequence of events. The two observers, standing in what they believe to be a haunted house, hear a rustling noise. They decide to search for its source, with the possibility of a paranormal origin in mind. On reaching the floor below the only thing visible is the sack of coal, with a stain at some distance from it. One of the observers thinks he recalls having seen the stain right next to the sack before, and puts this interpretation to the other one, who concurs at least to the extent of considering it a serious possibility. It is reported as such to Price, who reinforces this interpretation; with the passage of time such doubts as may have lingered at the time of the incident vanish, and another mystery has been created. As I have emphasized, this account is mere speculation. On the other hand, when this incident was described in a lecture fifteen years after it happened, a characteristic elaboration was introduced; it was stated that the sack had been ringed with chalk. This makes the story more plausible as evidence of the paranormal but by the same token testifies to its tenuous nature as originally reported.

A further discussion of these factors will be pursued in a later chapter. Here we turn to the processes of influence at work in small groups, to which a great deal of study has been devoted during the past two decades. As some of the most spectacular of the alleged phenomena have taken place in small groups, characteristic of the seance room, this work is clearly relevant. In the past, critics have usually pointed to the physical conditions, for example the low level of illumination, as one likely source of error. However, certain studies indicate that the psychological process involved in small groups may be equally important.

The studies of Asch, an American social psychologist, and his followers were concerned with the effect exerted upon an individual's judgement of hearing the judgements of others. The object to be judged was a physical one, namely the comparative lengths of sets of lines. The task was clear-cut, and people performing it individually made practically no errors. The experiment was set up so that the group of subjects contained several stooges who were instructed to give a series of wrong judgements. Things were arranged in such a way that the one subject in the group who had not been told what was going on was the last to respond, so that the clear evidence of his own eyes was pitted against what he believed to be the direct experience of others witnessing the same stimuli. In the event, it was shown by Asch, and has been repeatedly confirmed since, that a great many people will tend to respond in the same way as the rest of the group.

Many of the so-called 'yielders' do so because they wish to avoid being regarded as peculiar, and may in private stick to their own convictions; others manage to persuade themselves that they 'see' what the rest of the group apparently sees. There are thus, under certain conditions, tremendous pressures on an individual to fall into line with the remainder of his fellows; and these are likely to be even more potent when the stimulus is not a straightforward one like the length of lines, but diffuse and ambiguous like the phenomena in the seance room, or the weird performances of cult-priest or magician. Moreover, in the latter cases there is usually a will to believe. Strong expectations are aroused that certain extraordinary things are going to happen, and under such circumstances slight perceptual cues are readily interpreted in accordance with such expectations.

It may be asked at this point: what about the sceptic and scoffer, is he not going to destroy such an edifice of illusion? The first answer, which will be somewhat elaborated subsequently, is that it is not easy outside modern industrial cultures to become a sceptic. Secondly, another characteristic of group behaviour, first demonstrated by Schachter, is relevant here. He showed that in the presence of a dissenter, members of a group will unite to bring their persuasive powers to bear on him so as to make him change his mind and toe the line. If he fails to do so, he may be cast out from the group, and in a pre-industrial society this can be a catastrophic fate. There are thus strong psychological mechanisms operating to preserve uniformity of belief, even where this belief be superstition and error.

Before concluding I shall relate a personal experience illustrating how powerful the effects of expectations can be. A good many years ago I found myself in the company of six other people after dinner, and the conversation veered towards the supernatural. An impromptu seance was proposed, and all of us settled around a large circular table. The idea was that questions would be asked, and the spirits would answer by rapping once for 'yes' and twice for 'no'. The first question was asked, but nothing happened. We sat for several minutes in the semi-darkness, with tension rising. Getting rather stiff, I shifted in my chair, accidentally knocking the table, and was staggered to find that this was taken as the expected answer. After a brief struggle with my conscience, the desire to experiment gained the upper hand; I told myself that after a while I would reveal the deception and pass it off as a joke. For another half-hour or so I knocked the table quite blatantly with the tip of my shoes, without arousing the slightest suspicion. I was just about to summon up courage to come clean, when one of the persons present asked the spirit to materialize. Another long tense silence followed, then one person whispered, 'He's there, in the corner – a little grey man'. It was said with such conviction that I almost expected to see something when I looked. There was in fact nothing except a faint shadow cast by a curtain moving in a slight breeze. Two others claimed to see the homunculus quite clearly; and it was explained to the rest that they lacked the necessary second sight. With this climax the seance ended, and the moment for a possible confession was irrevocably past.

There is a postscript to this story. About a year after the seance I met one of the participants. Recalling the evening, he said that he had previously been sceptical about the occult, but this experience had convinced him. On hearing this my guilt feelings were thoroughly aroused, and I decided to make a clean breast of it. Once more I had badly miscalculated – he just would not believe me. The way he seemed to see it was that in the cold light of day I had reverted to the role of hard-boiled psychologist, and felt the need to explain everything away. Although this was by no means my only object-lesson of how readily perceptual error occurs, and how persistent beliefs can be in the face of evidence, it was certainly the most dramatic one.

If superstition were merely the result of error, be it of perception, memory or judgement, it ought to be relatively easy to correct. In fact, people hardly ever abandon such beliefs as a result of rational argument. If superstition were merely determined by social pressures, their removal ought to dispel superstition; this is sometimes true, but not invariably: there are people who cling tenaciously to their superstitions. It looks as though they had strong roots within the personality of the individual, and theories grappling with this problem will now be examined.

REFERENCES

1 F. Engels, 'Dialects of Nature', in K. Marx and F. Engels, *On Religion*, Moscow: Foreign Languages Publishing House, 1958, p. 176.

2 Wilhelm Wundt, *Elements of Folk Psychology*, Allen & Unwin, 1916, p. 93.

3 Alfred Lehmann, *Aberglaube und Zauberei*, Stuttgart: Enke, 1898.

4 P. H. Benson, *Religion in Contemporary Culture*, New York: Harper, 1960, p. 537.

5 So named by Colin Cherry (*On Human Communication*, New York: Wiley, 1957).

6 A. I. Hallowell, 'Cultural factors in the structuralization of perception', in J.H. Rohrer and M. Sherif (eds), *Social Psychology at the Crossroads*, New York: Harper, 1951.

7 *Remembering*, Cambridge University Press, 1932.

8 D. J. West, *Psychical Research Today*, Duckworth, 1954.

9 E. J. Dingwall, K. M. Goldney and T. H. Hall, *The Haunting of Borley Rectory*, Society for Psychical Research, 1956. It should perhaps be pointed out that this exposé has by no means convinced the believers; for instance Nando Fodor (*Between Two Worlds*, New York: Parker, 1964) wrote, 'No greater scandal has ever erupted in psychical research than over this preposterous exposure' (p. 184).

10 E. Rignano, *The Psychology of Reasoning*, New York: Harcourt Brace, 1923, p. 326.

11 Leon Festinger, 'A theory of social comparison processes', *Human Relations*, 1954, 7, 117-40.

CHAPTER FOUR

Superstition
and the Unconscious

If the word 'subliminal' is offensive to any of you, as smelling too much of psychical research or other aberrations, call it by any other name you please, to distinguish it from the level of full sunlit consciousness. Call this latter the A-region of personality, if you care to, and call the other the B-region. The B-region, then, is obviously the larger part of each of us, for it is the abode of everything that is latent and the reservoir of everything that passes unrecorded or unobserved. It contains, for example, such things as all our momentarily inactive memories, and it harbours the springs of all our obscurely motivated passions, impulses, likes, dislikes, and prejudices. Our intuitions, hypotheses, fancies, superstitions, persuasions, convictions, and in general all our non-rational operations, come from it.

William James *The Varieties of Religious Experience*

One of Freud's patients once related to him what she thought had been a prophetic dream. It was about meeting the former family doctor in front of a certain store. When she went to town the following day she did actually come across him at precisely the spot that had appeared in the dream. Freud had examined her story carefully, and it turned out that she had no recollection of the dream prior to the encounter with the physician. He therefore concluded that it was probably in the course of the meeting that she gained the conviction of having had the dream. Now one might say that here is an example of someone getting a superstitious notion because her memory had played her a trick.

However, Freud was not content to leave it at that. In his view such lapses of memory, errors of speech or writing and so on are not merely accidental occurrences, but can be demonstrated to be subject to a law if one acquires sufficient information about the psychological processes of the person concerned. His work on the *Psychopathology of Everyday Life*, from which this example is drawn, surveys a large array of cases of this kind.[1]

The next step was therefore to try and discover what had caused the powerful impression of having had a dream, and for this purpose Freud used his analytic method to discover the free associations of the patient. It emerged in the course of this analysis that she was emotionally attached to a man who was also a friend of the old family doctor. The ardour had cooled on his side, and on the day prior to the supposed dream he had failed to keep a date with her. Freud summed up his interpretation thus: '. . . her illusion, when she saw her friend of former days, of having had a prophetic dream was equivalent to some such remark as this: "Ah, doctor, you remind me now of past times, when I never had to wait in vain for N. if we'd arranged a meeting." ' (p. 263.)

The analysis of this case illustrates Freud's method, which he applied to superstition as well as other areas of mental functioning. He delved into the emotional life of his patients and, courageously and honestly, quite often into his own, in order to discover the law which he believed determined actions previously dismissed as chance events. However, the connexions that have to be uncovered before such an occurrence can be understood are apt to be devious. For instance, a man trying to recite a well-known poem was unable to recall the words 'with the white sheet'. Free associations to these words produced the following chain: white sheet on corpse – a close friend whose brother died recently of heart disease – he was very fat – my friend is fat too, might die of the same disease – news of this death frightened me since obesity runs in my family – my grandfather died of heart disease – I am rather stout as well and started a slimming cure a few days ago. Thus the reason why the man was unable to recall these words from a familiar poem was not that they had disappeared from his memory store; they were blocked from rising into his consciousness because of their associations with a threatening thought, the fear of death.

Freud interpreted superstitions in a similar manner. His first formulation, in *Psychopathology of Everyday Life*, places most emphasis on thoughts, fears and wishes which are present in a person's unconscious; owing to the fact that they are unacceptable to the ordinary everyday self (through being terrifying, painful, hostile, cruel, or otherwise socially rejected) they cannot gain access to what William James called 'full sunlit consciousness'. Nonetheless, these elements being actively present within the psyche, they are as it were clamouring to be allowed some outlet. According to Freud, one way in which their threat is dealt with is by attributing them to the outside world; this is called the mechanism of 'projection'. Thus in a person's unconscious there may be a cruel thought, even a death wish, directed against someone else, often a consciously loved person. This may then become translated into a premonition of death of the loved one; or, following an even more circuitous path, the guilt aroused by such an unworthy wish could lead to an expectation of punishment, and this in turn would manifest itself in a superstitious notion of misfortune threatening oneself.

In his later thinking on this problem Freud was influenced by his experience of the treatment of an obsessional neurotic who has come to be known as the 'rat-man'. The label is derived from this man's major anxiety, concerning a cruel punishment said to have been practised in the East. This consisted of a pot filled with rats being tied to the buttocks of the offender, which thereupon ate their way into the body. There is no need to dwell on the details of the case, whose interest in the present context lies in the fact that the rat-man had some strong personal superstitions of the kind mentioned in the earlier classification of types. They are best described in Freud's own words:

Our patient was to a high degree superstitious, and this although he was a highly educated and enlightened man of considerable acumen, and although he was able at times to assure me that he did not believe a word of all this rubbish. Thus he was at once superstitious and not superstitious; and there was a clear distinction between his attitude and the superstition of uneducated people who feel themselves at one with their belief. He seemed to understand that his superstition was dependent upon his obsessional thinking, although at times he gave way to it completely.[2]

The distinction here between different kinds of superstition is important, though Freud does not seem to have developed it systematically. One is the kind passively absorbed, as it were, from one's social environment, the other a response to pressing inner needs. The rat-man obviously belonged to the latter category, and one of the most striking features of his superstition was the notion of the *omnipotence* of his own thoughts, feelings and wishes. Since this at first sight appears an extraordinary notion, it may be as well to illustrate it concretely. On being challenged by Freud to offer some grounds for his convictions, the rat-man related among others the following experience: he went to a hydropathic establishment, where he enjoyed the favours of one of the nurses. Returning there for a second visit, he asked to be given the same room, next to that of the complaisant nurse. As it happened, the room was already occupied by an old professor, and on hearing this he thought, 'I wish he may be struck dead for it!' A fortnight later the professor had a stroke and died.

Now there is of course not necessarily anything miraculous about this. Most of us from time to time harbour unkind thoughts about our fellow-men, and some of them will after a shorter or longer interval succumb to disease or death. The question is why this should, in certain persons, produce a conviction of the omnipotence of their thoughts. Freud, in *Totem and Taboo*,[3] traces this back to the sexual development of early childhood, when part of the libido attaches itself to the emerging ego; in this narcissistic stage the efficacy of one's own psychic processes in affecting the outer world is vastly overestimated. Whilst in normal people this stage is largely, though not entirely, outgrown, it persists strongly in certain neurotics and leads them to ascribe external effects to their own thoughts and wishes. Freud believed that this persistence of narcissism is also characteristic of 'savages' and accounts for their magical beliefs. One of Freud's followers, Ferenczi, developed this idea further, pointing out that during the first year of life the infant's gestures, like his crying, actually do achieve their object. In this manner the infant is said to acquire the feeling that it controls the outside world.

How far does this theory contribute to our understanding of superstition? The answer will have to be a very roundabout one. The major difficulty one faces arises often with psychoanalysis: its propositions are equally difficult to verify and to falsify. In order to illustrate this problem, let us examine one of the cases Freud quotes in his chapter on 'Determinism, Chance and Superstitious Beliefs'. He is concerned to demonstrate that when we think of a number, the one that comes up is not as we usually assume random, but on the contrary relates in a clearly determined way to our personal life experiences and emotional problems.

Indeed, even those numbers which a person uses especially often in a particular connexion, in an apparently arbitrary way, can be traced by analysis to an unexpected meaning. Thus it struck a patient of mine one day that when annoyed he was especially fond of saying: 'I've told you that already from 17 to 36 times', and he asked himself whether there was any motive for it. It at once occurred to him that he was born on the 27th day of the month whereas his younger brother was born on the 26th, and that he had reason to complain that fate had so often robbed him of the good things in life in order to bestow them on his younger brother. He therefore represented this partiality on the part of fate by deducting ten from the date of his own birthday and adding it to his brother's. 'I am the elder and yet I am cut short like this.'[4]

On reading this, it seems plausible enough, but then comes the nagging suspicion that at another time, or with another analyst, the patient might well have come up with an entirely different though equally convincing set of reasons. Some of the psycho-analytic enthusiasts of number symbolism have carried this kind of interpretation to quite extraordinary lengths. An outstanding one is Paneth,[5] whose ingenuity is remarkable, if at times somewhat tortuous. One could make use of one of his schemes to give Freud's case a new look. On grounds which would be far too lengthy to elucidate, Paneth helpfully provides a key to the symbolic meaning of the relevant numbers:

$$\text{powers of } 2 = \text{psychoanalysis}$$

$$\text{powers of } 3 = \text{psychosynthesis}$$
$$\text{number } 17 = \text{complex}$$

Armed with this information, we can now give a new meaning to the phrase 'from 17 to 36'. The second number, it will be noted, breaks up into $2^2 \cdot 3^2$; it then becomes immediately obvious that the patient is saying: 'I suffered from a complex, but with the help of psychoanalysis I shall achieve psycho-synthesis and be cured.' This is not merely a joke, or if it is then the term is used in Freud's sense of intended criticism by con-densation of the central idea.

Several of Freud's followers have also written about super-stition. In so far as they wrote about particular forms of it, and seemed unaware of the work of their colleagues, one can assess the extent to which their interpretations are in agreement. Thus both Fliess[6] and Marmor[7] published papers dealing mainly with the superstitious practice of 'knocking on wood'. Marmor's paper appeared some twelve years later, and he did not refer to his predecessor. Let us look at both these accounts.

Fliess treats it as a prototype of a magical ritual, and gives a description of the action:

One of the most widespread magical activities practised in the modern world is 'knocking on wood'. Classically, the gesture is per-formed three times with the knuckle of the bent index finger, preferably on a table, window-sill, or the like, with an approach from below. The very persons who most loudly proclaim their freedom from super-stition are most devout in observing this ritual. While they look about for a suitable, i.e. unquestionably wooden, object, they accompany a more or less graceful attitude of detachment with a smile of indulgence. They must knock on wood lest Fate reverse the favourable state of affairs with which they have just expressed satisfaction. (p. 328.)

The sheepishness with which people are apt to perform such magical rituals is shrewdly observed, and it is evident that there is a very real problem here: why do sensible well-educated people behave like this in the twentieth century?

The answer given by Marmor is that if 'fate', 'God' (in Christianity) or the 'gods' (in classical mythology) demand humility from man, this is because all these are parent surrogates. In other words, the fear arises from a persistence of feelings experienced towards parents during childhood. In part these are said to be the result of the oedipal phase, whereby the child comes into conflict, at least in fantasy, with the parent of opposite sex; more generally, parents of either sex have to curb the impulses of their offspring, who are not free to express their hostility towards the sources of frustration because of their dependence upon them. Self-assertiveness is thus suppressed, and the adult manifesting it experiences a fleeting anxiety that has to be allayed.

Apart from this factor of parental authority, Marmor sees another source in the competitive aspects of Western social structure. Being better than others is apt to produce envy and hostility on the part of rivals. In order to avoid this, people tend to minimize their own prosperity and good fortune. Marmor quotes many familiar examples of this, showing how people play down the worth of their new acquisitions or magnify their difficulties ('Yes, it's a nice car, but I don't know how I'm going to pay for it'). He cites a connected superstition which emerged from a study of pregnant women, many of whom apparently refrain from buying a layette before the seventh or eighth month, for fear that something might happen. Marmor goes on to describe a clinical syndrome of 'fear of success', showing how people suffering from this fall prey to severe anxiety when achieving success; and he gives details of one such case where knocking on wood had become a compulsive ritual.

While Marmor's discussion is full of interest, placing the problem in a historical context, it cannot be said that he has really come to grips with the question why the knocking on wood should afford relief from anxiety. Fliess starts off in a similar vein, stating that 'the individual is forced to perform this ritual by a fearful tension, produced by the anticipation of aggression at the hands of "fate" (formerly the parents)'. However, he views this as a superficial interpretation, and proposes that one must seek for an explanation in a deeper psychic layer, reaching back to the pre-oedipal period in infancy. According to him, the symbolism of the ritual can be expressed in three equations: wood=mother; finger=penis; three=male genitalia. The interpretation is best conveyed in Fliess' own words:

She, the mother (womb), is approached from below, and with an ambivalent attitude towards castration: the subject's own phallic genital is denied (the bent finger) and at the same time affirmed (the three knocks). The 'knocking' itself can only be an intended destruction and impregnation.

What Fliess is saying is that certain powerful though inchoate impulses surviving since infancy manifest themselves in certain situations characterized by an oral transgression. This leads to feelings of anxiety, which are dispelled by a ritual charged with profound symbolism whereby some of these infantile strivings are given indirect expression. In support of this interpretation Fliess presents clinical cases, concerned with the unusual sexual behaviour and fantasies of two women patients. As in much psychoanalytic discussion, these constitute evidence only if a whole set of assumptions are already accepted; to a sceptical outsider, they fail to carry conviction, because as already indicated earlier not only the detailed interpretation of symbols, but the more general account of phenomena, is apt to vary from one psychoanalytic writer to another. This is not to say that the different accounts are usually contradictory, or even fundamentally inconsistent. Thus in the present case there is but a slight overlap between the explanations proffered by Marmor and Fliess, yet both might well be valid. The objection is that each of them appears to consider his own explanation a necessary and sufficient one.

These critical observations should not be allowed to obscure the merit of psychoanalysts in raising some extremely important questions concerning the relationship between superstitious ideas or beliefs and mental illness. Certain facts are beyond dispute, having been noted by all those who deal with the mentally ill, irrespective of whether they are enthusiastic adherents or bitter opponents of psychoanalysis. Neurotics often exhibit in grossly exaggerated form the kind of beliefs and overt behaviour one would normally characterize as superstitious, and they experience an overpowering compulsion to do so. Here is a typical case reported by Odier,[8] which ends with an ironical twist.

G. is a highly intelligent student who was reading for a degree in philosophy. Here he is getting ready to leave for his oral examination.

Going out of his place, he opens and closes the door three times. Downstairs he touches the handle of the outer door seven times. On the way he uses the tip of his stick to push anything lying on the pavement into the gutter. On arrival at the Sorbonne he goes once again through his regressive performances, opening and closing the entrance door three times, then touching seven times the handle of the door leading to the lecture theatre. This done, all will go well; he is quite certain of it. Entering the candidates' room boldly, he faces his examiners and answers their questions brilliantly . . . Fate in its malice decreed that he was to be questioned on problems of psychology!

It is evident that a knowledge of psychology does not help the victim of such a compulsion, which stems from elements within his personality over which he has no control. Odier, like several other writers concerned with this problem, traces it back to fear. Natural in all children in certain situations, he holds there are some perhaps constitutionally more prone to it. Such a child is apt to attribute evil intentions to those who thwart his impulses, and the fear turns into anxiety which leads to the world being perceived as dangerous and threatening in the absence of any objective justification. Among the several ways of coping with this state, described by Odier, is superstition. In his discussion Odier claims that such neurotics develop a defence against the felt threats by simply endowing various objects and gestures with magical power. Like the small child who cannot bear going to sleep without his pet toy, so the anxiety neurotic of this type relies on mascots, amulets or such gestures as 'touching wood'. Actually from the examples given by Odier it is clear that as often as not the person merely adopts a superstition prevalent in his social environment, but makes it his own in a manner highly charged with emotion.

If one discusses their behaviour with such people, they tend to rationalize it:

If I keep this good-luck charm on my desk . . . I am all right and work well. Anyway, one never knows! It is therefore better for me to believe in these charms than not to believe; it is better to 'touch wood' than not to touch it . . .

From their own point of view this position, like Pascal's famous wager, has something to commend itself. Yet it is apparent in well-educated patients, as Freud had already stressed, that they are not of one mind; it seems as though they are trying to convince themselves. Part of them is frankly sceptical, and somewhat ashamed; another part, the dominant one in neurotics, firmly believes.

In some types of more severe mental illness, like acute schizophrenia, the rational element may be almost entirely in abeyance, patients living the whole of their mental life in an atmosphere of unrelieved magic. They may believe either in (to the normal) fantastic threats from the outside, or that they themselves enjoy vast magical powers, or a combination of both. The feeling of omnipotence to which Freud alluded may be present full-blown. Thus a patient may think it his job to keep the sun in its place, that he can make new bodies for other people, or control the world. More often, perhaps, it is the magical threats from the outside that are being feared: devils who put poison in their food, spirits that suck out their vital substance, or mysterious machines that are being used to influence and usually damage them. These symptoms have received a great deal of attention in the psychiatric literature, and it would be beyond the scope of this essay to survey them. The chief interest here lies in the resemblance between many of these symptoms of mental patients in Western industrialized countries and the beliefs of normal people in other cultures. Roheim, who was both an anthropologist and a psychoanalyst, made this point very strongly:

Schizophrenics frequently affirm that they are being beaten or burnt, that their heads are being turned backward, that their legs are being made shorter, and that their eyes are being pulled out (with the empty sockets being visible in a mirror). Food disappears from their stomachs; their testicles are swollen; any and every organ has been removed, inverted, or cut to pieces; or their lungs are inflated because a fat gentleman has been sucked into the body via the genitalia.

All this sounds exactly like primitive magic. These are the things that the normal primitive fears; these are the things that he believes a sorcerer can do to him.[9]

This parallel raises a difficult question of origins, which Roheim seeks to answer in terms of universal developmental trends along Freudian lines. This runs roughly as follows: infants pass through a fantasy stage in their process of adaptation to reality; psychoses involve a regression of this earlier stage on the part of adults; the 'primitive' when he makes use of magic draws his beliefs from that same early stage. Roheim, as an experienced anthropologist, goes beyond Freud in his awareness that magic in pre-literate societies is a socially shared ritual; but he fails to resolve the problems posed thereby. Unlike the spontaneous creations of psychotics, the magical acts of a medicine man, for instance, are on the whole socially prescribed and transmitted by tradition; does it make sense, therefore, to interpret them in terms of the particular individual's infantile experiences? And if not, to whose experiences should they be referred?

From quite a different non-Freudian standpoint Field[10] has put forward the view that original schizophrenic fantasies have historically been the source of magical ideas. She suggests that people whose illness was not recognized as such in their culture were responsible for propagating them, supporting her case with field studies in West Africa together with parallels in British mental hospitals. Thus, starting from the similarities that so impressed Roheim, she reaches a rather different conclusion, whose weakness is that it fails to account for the surprising acceptance of such fantastic notions by normal people.

These are difficult questions, which have not been satisfactorily resolved. There are indications that important relationships exist between individual symbolism and that of social rituals, but its nature remains obscure. Leach, an anthropologist, has discussed the problem in an illuminating essay.[11] He took as his starting point a study by Berg, a psychoanalyst, on the symbolism of hair.[12] On the basis of clinical work with Western patients Berg came to the conclusion that head hair is a symbol of the genitals. It follows that hair-cutting or shaving constitute symbolic 'castration' and, more widely, an attempt to control primary aggressive impulses. Berg himself strove to support his argument for the universality of this symbolism by quoting some rather old-fashioned ethnographic material. Leach, casting his net far wider, marshals impressive evidence from most parts of the world which seems to fit in remarkably well with Berg's contention. It also makes good 'common' sense if one thinks of the

63

+ one could argue precisely the reverse.

x monk's tonsure or the uncut hair of the contemporary beatniks. Leach demonstrates that individual symbolism is consistent with social ritual, much of which is magical in character; and he argues that the ritual is effective because it evokes unconscious symbols in the participants. What remains to be shown is that the symbolism is in fact universal, and if so how the remarkable fit between personal symbolism and social ritual came to develop.

The other great depth psychologist, Jung, would probably have regarded this approach to the problem as wrong-headed. He was so impressed by the similarity of symbolism in different parts of the world that he used this as the basis for inferring that there exists a *collective* unconscious in which all human beings share. This is a difficult notion to swallow for more tough-minded psychologists, including Freud, because it is hard to see how it could either be proved or disproved. In many ways the two men were poles apart, and this was true of the manner in which they dealt with superstition. While Freud occasionally toyed with the idea that there might be genuinely occult phenomena,[13] he generally assumed the falsity of superstitions, making it his business to analyse the psychological processes responsible along the lines already discussed. Jung, in contrast, had a more open attitude to the whole subject, though it is not easy to pin him down. This is because Jung's writings are couched in somewhat ambiguous language, and the concepts he used are apt to be very elusive – perhaps they had to be in order to do justice to the subtle complexities of his subject-matter. At any rate, he refused to acknowledge any sharp dichotomy between true and false beliefs, taking the view that superstitions fulfil certain functions in human life:

> Our religious and political ideologies are methods of salvation and propitiation which can be compared with primitive ideas of magic, and when such 'collective representations' are lacking their place is immediately taken by all sorts of private idiocies and idiosyncrasies, manias, phobias and daemonisms whose primitivity leaves nothing to be desired, not to speak of psychic epidemics of our time before which the witch-hunts of the sixteenth century pale by comparison.[14]

Jung is saying here that nowadays we rely on other sets of beliefs to cater for basically the same need; and if society fails to provide us with socially shared objects of belief the substitutes to which we are led to resort are a good deal worse. This is not just a variant of a fairly common idea, typified by a remark of Masaryk's to the effect that people today are as anthropomorphic about politics as their ancestors about nature. This implies a certain optimism – we have moved far in our mastery of nature, but have not yet caught up in understanding and controlling human society. Jung would have regarded this as an illusion; from his perspective the subterranean forces of the collective unconscious will never be subject to full rational control; and at the deepest level there is really nothing much to choose between our cherished political or religious ideologies and magical ideas which so readily take their place. Although again Jung is not explicit about this, one gains the impression that he does not so much wish to depreciate politics and religion as to appreciate superstition. In any case he treats superstition as a fundamental attribute of the human psyche, and few of his massive volume of writings fail at least to touch upon it. A comprehensive review being out of the question, one particular contribution will be selected to bring out some salient features of his thinking. This is based on a lecture delivered to the Society for Psychical Research, entitled 'The Psychological Foundations of Belief in Spirits'.[15]

Jung begins by stating that, in spite of the rationalism of the last century and a half, beliefs in spirits and similar manifestations remain widespread among people at large. At a higher intellectual level, he welcomed the revival of interest in such questions by eminent men like Crookes and Myers (associated with the SPR), on the grounds that this helps to free the thinking of educated people from 'materialistic dogmas'. It has been a constant theme in Jung's writings that people nowadays are excessively rationalistic, and thus deny an outlet to an important part of their nature, which then may find sudden violent expression. He contrasts this with the world of the 'primitive', who is fully alive to both material and spiritual reality, and for whom indeed spirits are direct evidence of the reality of the spiritual world. He raises the question whether apparitions and ghosts are in fact more commonly seen among primitives than Europeans. His somewhat ambiguous answer is that 'psychic phenomena'

65

occur with equal frequency among Europeans, but the latter make much less use of the 'spirit hypothesis'. He goes so far as to say: 'I am convinced that if a European had to go through the same exercises and ceremonies which the medicine-man performs in order to make the spirits visible, he would have the same experiences.' (p. 303.)

At this point it is perhaps worth interrupting the exposition, since I am able to offer some comments based on personal participation in rituals. Some years ago a medicine-man in West Africa described to me the procedures which made it possible for him to see spirits. Like Jung, he suggested that if I underwent the same regime, they would become visible to me as well. To his delighted astonishment I declared my readiness to do so. There is no need to dwell on the details of the procedure which were certainly onerous; for instance, I had to kill a cock, mix its blood with medicine powder he had given me, and smear this on my forehead every night for a fortnight. Although it involved, to put it mildly, a good deal of inconvenience, I scrupulously went through every motion. But alas, when I went on the appointed night to the bush where the spirits were supposed to reveal themselves, they failed to keep the appointment. When I complained, the medicine-man's characteristic explanation was that I must have missed out something from one of the stages. That time, with one particular European, going through the same exercises did not result in the promised experience.

On another occasion, the outcome was more positive. The priest of a cult undertook to demonstrate to me the power of his god, and for this purpose I had to take part in a ritual dance. Guided by one of his acolytes, and instructed under no circumstances to let go of the slippery bottom end of a cleft stick, I was rushed around to the increasingly frantic beat of the drums. With the noise, excitement and fatigue most of the participants went into a trance after some time, and it was only by exerting a great effort to keep detached and maintain to some extent my purpose as an observer that I avoided experiencing the power of the god.

Judging from this, and other people's reports, what Jung claims is only partly true; under certain circumstances a European may share the same experiences, but this does not mean that they were necessarily supernatural ones. However, let us return from this digression to Jung's account of what he considered three main sources from which belief in spirits springs: apparitions, dreams and pathological states. The first is not quite as tautologous as it might seem, for it is explained with reference to Jung's concept of 'autonomous complexes'; these are regarded as unconscious parts of the psyche detached from the self, which do not reach the level of awareness. They can, however, be projected on to the outside world, and then appear as spirits. This interpretation appears to have certain elements in common with that of Freud, but the difference between the two men comes out clearly in a footnote where Jung stresses that psychology does not really concern itself with the problems as to whether spirits exist *in themselves* (Jung's italics). He goes on to show that the primitive theory of causation of illness through loss of soul or possession by spirits is in some ways closely parallel to his own theory of causation. For instance, he discusses his distinction between the individual and collective unconscious, pointing out that the primitive notion of souls corresponds to the former, and that of spirits to the latter.

The collective unconscious is affected by the social, political or religious conditions of a society. External changes are often preceded by activation of the contents of the collective unconscious, which while preparing individuals for a transformation are also a source of mental disturbance and may lead to people mistaking the contents of the collective unconscious for reality – a pathological state. According to Jung:

Spirits are complexes of the collective unconscious which appear when the individual loses his adaptation to reality, or which seek to replace the inadequate attitude of a whole people by a new one. They are therefore either pathological fantasies or new but as yet unknown ideas. (p. 315.)

Unless one has a thorough acquaintance with Jung's thought (and sometimes even then) all this may be far from clear. Unless I have totally misunderstood him, there are several objections that might be raised against such an interpretation. The main one is that spirits are regularly reported as being seen on certain ritual occasions, without either any impending radical social changes or

67

any evidence of pathology on the part of the perceivers Moreover, Jung extends the same line of argument to fears of ghosts of the dead, which he assumed to be universal; but there is evidence indicating that this is a false assumption, and in fact the circumstances leading to the presence or absence of such fears can to some extent be specified.[16]

When Jung first delivered this lecture, he ended by expressing the opinion that there is no proof of the real existence of spirits. In a later edition he added a footnote stating that experiences over many years had led him to change his mind, and he now felt such phenomena were definitely established. In his autobiographical work[17] he describes many personal experiences, particularly of prophetic dreams. One relating to an apparition is worth quoting, as it typifies Jung's curious attitude in such matters.

One night I lay awake thinking of the sudden death of a friend whose funeral had taken place the day before. I was deeply concerned. Suddenly I felt that he was in the room. It seemed to me that he stood at the foot of my bed and was asking me to go with him. I did not have the feeling of an apparition; rather, it was an inner visual image of him, which I explained to myself as a fantasy. But in all honesty I had to ask myself, 'Do I have any proof that this is a fantasy? Suppose it is not a fantasy, suppose my friend is really here and I decided he was only a fantasy – would that not be abominable of me?' Yet I had equally little proof that he stood before me as an apparition. Then I said to myself, 'Proof is neither here nor there.' Instead of explaining him away as a fantasy, I might just as well give him the benefit of the doubt and for experiment's sake credit him with reality. (p. 289.)

He was always rather inclined to give the supernatural 'the benefit of the doubt', without undue concern for proof. It would probably not be unfair to regard him as superstitious, as at least one reviewer of this book did. Incidentally, the sequel to the above was that he followed the beckoning friend (in his imagination) to his house, where he showed him the location of a particular book in his library. Checking on this the following day Jung discovered the book was entitled *The Legacy of the Dead*, by Emile Zola. This rather disappointing dénouement reminds one of the caustic observation by Huxley that the departed do not appear to have much of interest to communicate. Yet although Jung was fond of moving in the obscure twilight zone which few other scholars care to penetrate, he did not confine himself to mere assertion. As might be expected from a man of his nature, he put forward an elaborate theoretical structure reaching out beyond the depth-psychological interpretations briefly described, which have at least a certain affinity with Freudian theory. We shall return to this in a subsequent chapter.

In spite of the sharp divergence between the positions of Freud and Jung in this sphere, they do have several things in common. Both agree that superstitious beliefs and practices are deeply rooted in man's unconscious mental processes; both held that superstition is not a thing of the past, or confined to the less educated – in fact it is regarded as part and parcel of everybody's mental make-up, liable to come to the surface under certain circumstances. The evidence on which both relied for their theoretical formulations consisted mainly of case histories of their patients. Above all, they stress the emotional element in superstition, which helps us to understand why confronting the superstitious person with contradictory information often makes so little difference.

REFERENCES

1 Sigmund Freud, *Collected Works*, vol. VI, Hogarth Press, 1960.
2 *Collected Works*, vol. X, Hogarth Press, 1955, p. 229.
3 *Collected Works*, vol. XIII, Hogarth Press, 1955.
4 *Collected Works*, vol. VI, p. 246.
5 L. Paneth, *La Symbolique des Nombres dans l'Inconscient*, Paris: Payot, 1953.
6 Robert Fliess, 'Knocking on wood. A note on the pre-oedipal nature of the "magic effect"', *Psychoanalytic Quarterly*, 1944, 13, pp. 327–40.
7 Judd Marmor, 'Some observations on superstitions in contemporary life', *American Journal of Orthopsychiatry*, 1956, 26, pp. 119–30.
8 Charles Odier, *L'angoisse et la pensée magique*, Neuchatel: Delachaux, 1947.
9 Geza Roheim, *Magic and Schizophrenia*, New York: International Universities Press, 1955, p. 102.
10 M. J. Field, *Search for Security*, Faber, 1960.
11 E. R. Leach, 'Magical hair', *Journal of the Royal Anthropological Institute*, 1958, 88, pp. 147–64.
12 Charles Berg, *The Unconscious Significance of Hair*, Allen & Unwin, 1951.
13 See Ernest Jones, *Sigmund Freud*, vol. 3, Hogarth Press, 1957, chapter 14, 'Occultism'.

14 C. G. Jung, *Collected Works*, vol. 5, Kegan Paul, 1956, p. 156.
15 *Collected Works*, vol. 8, Kegan Paul, 1956.
16 J. W. M. Whiting, 'Sorcery, Sin and the Superego', in M. R. Jones (ed.), *Nebraska, Symposium on Motivation*, Lincoln, Neb.: University of Nebraska Press, 1959.
17 C. G. Jung, *Memories, Dreams, Reflections*, Routledge, 1963.

CHAPTER FIVE

Superstition as a Conditioned Response

... the chance knowledge of the marvellous effects of gifted springs is probably as ancient as any sound knowledge is to medicine whatever. No doubt it was mere casual luck at first that tried these springs and found them answer. Somebody by accident tried them and by that accident was instantly cured. The chance which happily directed men in this one case, misdirected them in a thousand cases. Some expedition had answered when the resolution to undertake it was resolved on under an ancient tree, and accordingly that tree became lucky and sacred. Another expedition failed when a magpie crossed its path, and a magpie was said to be unlucky. A serpent crossed the path of another expedition, and it had a marvellous victory, and accordingly the serpent became a sign of great luck ...

The worst of these superstitions is that they are easy to make and hard to destroy. A single run of luck has made the fortune of many a charm and many idols.

Walter Bagehot *Physics and Politics*

If one were to arrange psychological theories on a continuum ranging from 'hard' to 'soft', then Jungian psychology would definitely be located towards the latter extreme, with psychoanalysis slightly harder but still close to it. More or less at the opposite pole one would find behaviourism, claiming a near-monopoly of scientific purity and rigour. Their respective approaches are in sharp contrast: psychoanalysis is founded largely on inferences from the verbal utterances of the mentally ill, behaviourism mainly on the behaviour of animals in experimental

71

situations. Extremists in both camps can see no good in the other; some behaviourists go so far as to regard psychoanalysis as a mythology, and believers in it as almost superstitious; Freudians in turn are apt to maintain that behaviourists are completely blind to the most fundamental problems of human life. A majority of psychologists are middle-of-the-roaders, taking what suits them from both. This is because their varying perspectives are not necessarily always contradictory. Human behaviour is extremely complex, and there are bound to be numerous ways of discovering orderly patterns among its multitudinous facets.

In fact, several excellent studies have been based on an eclectic marriage of psychoanalysis and behaviour theory, the ancestry of the less reputable partner being sometimes concealed. This was possible because a common element is shared among all psychological theories, namely the modification of behaviour as a result of experience; the major divergence concerns the specific manner in which this occurs. Thus Freud held that certain childhood experiences resulted in unconscious mental processes of which superstition is one particular external manifestation. Behaviour theorists treat such beliefs and practices as the outcome of learning, in much the same way as they account for all other forms of behaviour; except that in superstition the learning has in a sense gone wrong.

We must now examine the theories of behaviourists in some detail. Since they tend to be rather tough-minded characters, few of them have seriously tackled the problem of superstition. An outstanding exception is one of their most prominent exponents, Skinner; but in order to make his theory intelligible one must go further back and begin with Pavlov, the founding father. Pavlov's work with dogs is now widely known, and the term 'conditioning' has become part of everyday language, though in the somewhat loose sense of 'influencing'. Like Freudian psychoanalysis, it has also been taken over in literature; Aldous Huxley in *Brave New World*, George Orwell in *1984* and many recent science fiction writers have made use of the principles of conditioning, generally in context where control is being exerted over people. This is not unconnected with the widespread belief, for which there is no good evidence, that Pavlov's principles have been applied to 'brainwashing'. In fact Pavlov's studies were at the outset concerned with the mundane problem of digestion. He noticed that his dogs often secreted saliva not merely as a result of contact with food, but already at the sight of it or even at the sound of the keeper's footsteps. Accordingly, he devised careful experiments to ascertain the precise circumstances in which this occurred. The basic principle is very simple. You ring a bell, and put a piece of meat in the dog's mouth; it is the meat which causes salivation, since you have already ascertained that the bell alone fails to elicit it. You repeat this procedure a substantial number of times, let us say fifty; then you ring the bell without following it by meat, and yet salivation takes place. The meat, effective before the experiment began, was the *unconditioned stimulus*; the salivation resulting from this is called the *unconditioned reflex*; the sound of the bell, neutral at the outset, is the *conditioned stimulus*; and the salivation produced by this as opposed to the meat is the *conditioned reflex*.

When presented in this way, the whole business seems rather obvious. After all, people who have never heard of Pavlov know that the sound of a dinner gong, or perhaps a vivid still life portraying attractive food, is capable of making one's mouth water. It is easy to poke fun at the apparent pomposity of the demonstration, and in fact Bernard Shaw did just this in *The Adventures of a Black Girl in Her Search for God*. What the scoffer fails to grasp is the contribution made by Pavlov's epoch-making work to our understanding of the way in which behaviour is modified, and of the cerebral processes involved. Pavlov indeed subtitled his book on conditioned reflexes 'an investigation of the physiological activity of the cerebral cortex'. The modification of behaviour comes about by the substitution of a previously neutral stimulus for the initially effective one. The change occurs when the stimulus that is to be conditioned is repeatedly 'reinforced' by the unconditioned stimulus. This notion of 'reinforcement' is an important one that will recur in the discussion. With Pavlov, it always followed a particular stimulus. The experimental environment was restricted in such a way that all other kinds of stimulation were as far as possible excluded; the freedom of action of the organism was similarly circumscribed, the dogs being constrained in a harness. Thus one could be confident that only the particular variables investigated played any part in the conditioning process. This was achieved at the cost of rigidly programming the behaviour of the organism.

Skinner, while building on the insights of Pavlov, introduced a radically new idea. This was a linkage between *reinforcement* and a response as opposed to a stimulus. The reinforcement consists of either reward or punishment, both of which have the property of changing the probability that the particular response reinforced will recur under similar circumstances in future. Skinner coined the term 'operant' for this type of conditioning because, in his own words, it 'emphasizes the fact that the behaviour *operates* upon the environment to generate consequences'.[1] In contrast to Pavlovian, operant conditioning makes use of the spontaneous behaviour of the organism, selectively reinforcing certain elements of it. In practice, although not in theory, certain restrictions are necessary for experimental purposes. Thus if one wishes to condition pigeons to press a lever, it is necessary to confine the pigeon to a box containing little else except a lever connected with a food-dispensing device. On the other hand, with domesticated animals or humans it is quite possible to undertake operant conditioning within the normal environment, proceeding by successive approximation. If you want to teach your dog to run into a particular corner of the room you reward him the first time he goes a little way in the desired direction, gradually delaying the reward until further progress is made towards the corner, until the behaviour is firmly established. As far as human beings are concerned, Skinner gave his ideas a literary form in a novel entitled *Walden Two*, where he imaginatively develops the application of his principles to a utopian community. In the extract below Skinner voices his views through the words of the founder of the community:

We made a survey of the motives of the unhampered child and found more than we could use. Our engineering job was to preserve them by fortifying the child against discouragement. We introduce discouragement as carefully as we introduce any other emotional situation, beginning at about six months. Some of the toys in our air-conditioned cubicles are designed to build perseverance. A bit of a tune from a music box, or a pattern of flashing lights, is arranged to follow an appropriate response – say, pulling on a ring. Later the ring must be pulled twice, later still three or five or ten times. It's possible to build up fantastically perseverative behaviour without encountering frustration or rage.[2]

Now what has all this to do with superstition? Skinner first of all approaches this theme in connexion with Pavlov's conditioned reflexes, when he points out their evolutionary value in so far as they assist an organism's adaptation to change in its environment. This is useful in so far as the sets of stimuli recur regularly in situations affecting the well-being of the individual. Thus a conditioned fear to the sight of a boiling kettle is of permanent value to a child who has burnt its fingers. On the other hand there are numerous cases where the pairing of stimuli is temporary or accidental, and these according to Skinner may produce superstitions. He does not in fact give any example of this kind of superstition, but merely illustrates 'irrational' behaviour arising from this: a child frightened by a dog may fear all dogs, including friendly and harmless ones. It is by no means clear at this stage why one conditioned reflex should be categorized as superstition, and another as merely 'irrational'.

Skinner's earliest systematic exposition is to be found in a paper whose title sounds like a jest, though it is really perfectly serious: ' "Superstition" in the pigeon'.[3] There he describes an experiment where a pigeon is placed in a cage in which at certain predetermined intervals food becomes available for periods of five seconds. Unlike the situation described above in the extract from the novel, where only certain selected responses of the children were reinforced, with the pigeons it was left to chance what particular activity was in progress when the food appeared. Thus one bird happened to turn its head counterclockwise at the crucial time; the reinforcement strengthened the response, and it was repeated more often than other responses; this in turn of course ensured that it would be more frequently rewarded, and thus a kind of ritual turning came to be established. With another pigeon a specific kind of head movement happened to be singled out, but in some cases not sufficient fortuitous linkages occurred to produce a 'superstition'. Skinner comments: 'The bird behaves

x Total crop — thus "as if" appears
only in your analysis — of the of these
the title in the famil-

as if there were a causal relation between its behaviour and the
x presentation of food' (p. 171). Already in this article Skinner expressed the view that the same principle is applicable to humans,
and this is more fully developed in *Science and Human Behavior*.

He begins by explaining that operant conditioning in organisms,
including humans, does not depend upon any awareness of the
connexion between response and reinforcer. As shown by the
pigeon set-up, there is also no need for any regular link between
response and reinforcement, the only relevant characteristic
being a temporal sequence of response-reinforcement, however
brought about. Since organisms are permanently active while
they are alive, a reinforcer is always assumed to reinforce something, and a single potent reinforcement may have substantial
consequences. We now come to the definition: 'If there is only
an accidental connexion between the response and the appearance
of a reinforcer, the behaviour is called "superstitious".'[4]

Skinner argues that humans resemble pigeons in this respect.
While admitting that only a small fraction of accidental contingencies generate ritualistic practices of the superstitious type,
he insists that the same principle is involved. The first example
given is the finding of a banknote of substantial value while
walking through a park. 'Whatever we were doing, or had just
been doing, at the moment we found the bill must be assumed to
be reinforced.' Thus the probability of the following sets of
behaviours is likely to be increased: going for a walk; in the
particular park; keep eyes to the ground, etc. Skinner admits
both that this would be hard to prove in practice, and also that
it is not really a superstition, though it is a set of behaviours that
are unlikely to be 'functional' in the sense of seriously increasing
our chances of finding another banknote.

The second example given is more directly relevant to our
central theme, and will therefore be quoted in full:

Some contingencies which produce superstitious behavior are not
entirely accidental. A response is sometimes likely to be followed by a
consequence which it nevertheless does not 'produce'. The best
examples involve a type of stimulus which is reinforcing when removed.
The termination of a brief stimulus of this sort may occur at just the
right time to reinforce the behavior generated by its onset. The

aversive stimulus appears and the organism becomes active; the stimulus terminates, and this reinforces some part of the behavior. Certain illnesses, lamenesses, and allergic reactions are of such duration that *any* measure taken to 'cure' them is likely to be reinforced when the condition clears up. The measure need not actually be responsible for the cure. The elaborate rituals of non-scientific medicine appear to be explained by this characteristic of many forms of illness.[5]

This is the kind of way, Skinner argues, in which the normally useful mechanism of conditioning can go wrong, and the fewer the reinforcements required to alter the probability of a response, the greater the risk that a mere coincidence results in a superstition. Skinner anticipates an obvious objection by granting that superstition in human society as a rule involves verbal elements that are passed on through the generations. Nonetheless he insists that they must have started with accidental operant reinforcement and been subsequently sustained by similar ones. While this is not quite the whole story, it would perhaps be as well to pause here for a critical scrutiny.

If one reads only the earlier part of Skinner's exposition, one might get the impression that he has reached a solution to the question with which the first chapter of this book struggled in vain, namely an objective definition of superstition; this would be based on 'an accidental connexion between the response and the appearance of a reinforcer'. In fact, his own usage is not consistent with this, for on several occasions he is forced to describe the resulting behaviour as 'irrational' or 'ineffective' but not superstitious. Later in the same work Skinner is obliged to concede this, though the manner in which it is done raises further difficulties. He says:

There is . . . no absolute distinction between a superstitious and a non-superstitious response . . . the tendency to behave superstitiously necessarily increases as the individual comes to be more sensitively affected by single contingencies. Between the contingency which is observed only once in the life of the individual and the contingency which is inevitably observed there is a continuum which we cannot divide sharply at any point to distinguish between 'superstition' and 'fact'.[6]

This passage brings out clearly a confusion which runs right through Skinner's approach to the problem of superstition. He fails to distinguish between (a) a form of behaviour induced by the accidental sequence of response and reinforcement and (b) the belief that a causal connexion is involved. It is this confusion which leads him to write about 'superstition' in animals; and when he states that a pigeon behaves *as if* there were a causal relation between its behaviour and the presentation of food the confusion is worse confounded. The phrase is absurdly anthropocentric, the causality being imputed by the observer. At another level there does of course exist a clear causal texture, imposed by the experimenter himself, about which there is no mystery. In the case of the pigeon, there is no question that (a) alone applies, though the wording conveys more or less by innuendo that (b) is in some sense involved. It must be emphasized further that the distinction drawn by Skinner between 'superstition' and 'fact' is possible only in relation to (b).

If the importance of differentiating (a) and (b) is established, it also follows that Skinner's stress on the mere *frequency* of particular contingencies is inappropriate. This is shown most simply by an illustration. Suppose a man (presumably an Ancient Egyptian) performs a ritual every morning in his life in the belief that this causes the sun to rise. Here the response is invariably reinforced, yet today we would not hesitate to call this a superstition. On the other hand a man may shout loudly in the mountains once only, and an avalanche is dislodged; he believes that he has caused the event, and this may well be a fact.

Now it must be admitted that the example of the Ancient Egyptian may be regarded to some extent as cheating, since the ritual was very unlikely to have been an accidental response and was presumably the result of social transmission. In answer to this one could refer to Skinner's view that superstitions must have started originally in this manner, a contention that also needs examination.

Before doing so, a few words are necessary on the so-called process of extinction. When reinforcement ceases, a response decreases in frequency and eventually becomes extinct. How readily this happens will depend on the previous history of the organism; if only a few responses have been reinforced, extinction will be rapid, while consistent reinforcements over a lengthy period of time result in very slow extinction. Skinner illustrates this as follows:

For example, though we have been reinforced with an excellent meal in a new restaurant, a bad meal may reduce our patronage to zero; but if we have found excellent food in a restaurant for years, several poor meals must be eaten there, other things being equal, before we lose the inclination to patronize it again.[7]

We are now ready to return to Skinner's account of superstitious cures. The first thing one might query is the description of illness as a 'brief' stimulus, but let that pass. As a result of such an aversive stimulus, the organism becomes active, and when spontaneous recovery takes place any measure taken to effect a cure is likely to be reinforced. The difficulty here is that the organism engages in a wide variety of activities, so why is it that just the attempted superstitious 'cure' happens to be reinforced? Is it a mere coincidence, as Skinner implies? The answer is of course that humans, unlike pigeons, do actually have notions about causal relationships; therefore among the varied antecedents of the recovery they single out those they themselves had previously conceived as having the desired effect.

Skinner might well be prepared to grant this, as he admits the importance for humans of culturally transmitted verbal formulae; but he still argues that such formulae must have originated in mere accidental contingencies. Unrealistic though it may be, let us imagine such a primordial state where no socially shared ideas about illness and its cure exist, so that each individual is thrown back on his own resources. This would mean that a wide variety of disparate 'cures' exist, depending upon what each person happened to do prior to recovery. How could a tradition emerge from this? Since there are many 'cures' in the field, each at the outset randomly related to the illness, most of them will fail to work on more than one occasion and thus become readily extinct. On the other hand there may be some, again entirely as a result of accident, which do make some contribution, however slight, to recovery. Hence over a vast number of cases the probability of reinforcement will be directly proportional to the real causal effectiveness of some of these cures. Hence they will tend to be selected and embodied in tradition; on this view, the process has positive survival value. There is in fact evidence consistent with such an interpretation. Among the multitude of remedies used by indigenous healers of different kinds which have been investigated, a substantial number have been found to be pharmaceutically effective; at the same time the healers using them had no idea of the biochemical processes whereby they functioned. Quite apart from this one has to reckon with the *placebo* effect, whereby any attempt to deal with an illness frequently has some kind of beneficial result.

It should also be noted that rituals often take place at a time and under circumstances where reinforcement is likely owing to natural causes, as in the Egyptian example cited earlier; or again, rain-making ceremonies are usually held when the rainy season is due. All this is not readily explained in terms of a merely accidental conjunction, as Skinner would have it. Another aspect worth mentioning is that repeated failure of reinforcement does not necessarily lead to extinction, and the reasons for this will be considered later. Enough has been said to support the burden of the argument that reasoning from the pigeon to humans in the simple manner proposed by Skinner just will not do. Of course, if the human subject is put into a situation analogous to that of the pigeon in a box, he will behave in a similar manner. This has been done by Catania and Cutts,[8] who gave Harvard students a button-pressing task, with responses on only one of two buttons being reinforced. Since the causal pattern remained hidden from the subjects, they often did respond 'superstitiously' along the lines of sequences accidentally reinforced at an early stage of the trials. It is difficult, however, to think of any real-life human superstitions to which these results might be relevant.

There is one further sphere to which Skinner sought to apply his theoretical scheme, namely witchcraft:

A prototype of religious control arises when rare or accidental contingencies are used in the control of behavior of others. For example, we may 'blame' someone for an unfortunate event which was not actually the result of his behavior, although the temporary relationship was such that a contingency can be asserted. 'If you hadn't dawdled so, we should have started earlier, and the accident never would have happened.' We blame him in order to alter his future behavior – to make him less likely to dawdle, and we achieve this by converting an unrelated event into an effective punishing consequence through certain verbal processes. We use the event as a punishment, even though we did not actually arrange the contingency. *It is only a short step to claiming the ability to arrange such contingencies* [italics added]. This is the underlying principle of witchcraft.[9]

First of all it is appropriate to recognize the ingenuity of this analysis of behaviour control, which provides a rationale for a process with which everybody is familiar. Having said this, it is necessary to go on to point out that the phrase in italics is little more than a piece of verbal sleight-of-hand. What is called a short step here is in fact a vast and crucial one; for the possibility of being able to claim the power to arrange such contingencies *depends on the prior existence of superstitious beliefs*, i.e. the very beliefs supposedly accounted for by the theory. Actually, as will be shown in the next chapter, witchcraft can hardly be understood in psychological terms alone; it has to be examined as part of a social system at least as much as a characteristic of individuals, and Skinner is not even fully aware of the nature of the problem. Without such a wider perspective, his statement that control is exerted by the person 'claiming' to produce good or bad luck is merely trivial. The person performs a social role in which such a claim is often implicit, and the functioning of this wider system has to be elucidated if one is concerned with the problem of control.

Failure to draw clear distinctions between three levels of analysis, concerned respectively with animal behaviour, individual human behaviour and the functioning of a social system, is the greatest weakness of Skinner's approach, vitiating most of his conclusions. His thought has probably little to contribute towards our understanding of socially shared superstitions. On the other hand, he does provide an important key to the genesis of private superstitions, of the kind described by Carveth Read. The catching of a good fish reinforces not only the tendency to go back to the same place, but one is apt for a while to put on the same cap and pocket the same pipe one had on that happy occasion, all rationally irrelevant features. Gamblers often have elaborate private rituals that probably derive from whatever activity happened to be reinforced by a particular stroke of luck. I have myself observed the case of a person who won a large sum on the football pools, and encountered a black and white cat at the time the news arrived. For years afterwards there persisted a ritual of looking out for the cat when the pool results were due.

In general Skinner's interpretations do help towards an understanding of at least one limited though important facet of superstition. As is evident from the quotation at the head of this chapter, some of his basic ideas are not new, though he elaborated them into a more systematic form and provided a psychological rationale that was absent from Bagehot's work. The main weakness is the absence of any systematic empirical work other than the pigeon-type studies which, for the reasons suggested, can only be regarded as marginally relevant.

There is one study stemming from the same broad tradition, though following a line somewhat different from that of Skinner. This is the work of John Whiting,[10] a psychological anthropologist influenced by both Freudian and behaviour theory. His was a field study among a New Guinea tribe, and one of his objects was to examine the social transmission, as opposed to the origins, of supernatural beliefs. Among these are beliefs in ghosts, sorcery and huge monsters called *marsalai*. How are these beliefs inculcated? According to Whiting, the basic process is one of generalization from real dangers. The term 'generalization' is employed here in a technical sense: it means a conditioned response to a stimulus which only resembles the conditioned stimulus in certain respects, but is not identical with it. Taking this as his starting-point, Whiting drew a distinction between realistic and unrealistic warnings issued by those charged with guidance and controlling the behaviour of the young, to whom he refers in a broad sense as 'teachers'. A realistic warning is defined as one which, if not observed, will have as its outcome pain from the source specified; an unrealistic warning is one where no such consequences follow non-observance. Kwoma youngsters are constantly warned about dangers in both their natural and social environments. Here are some examples of realistic warnings: avoidance of poisonous foods (illness or death); respect for the property of others (punishment by the owner); not going alone in a swamp (danger from wild pigs or crocodiles); boys are not to stare at the genitals of females (who will punish them); girls are not to behave immodestly (they will be criticized). In this and numerous other cases of this type the chances are that the child who fails to take any notice of the warning will suffer the consequences forecast by the teacher. In this way a strong habit of observing warnings is created, which extends to non-existent dangers.

A more specific mechanism is that described by Clark Hull, one of the outstanding behaviour theorists, as 'secondary generalization'. When two or more objects are referred to by the same term, people will react to them in a similar way. In this particular case *marsalai* are described as great snakes or crocodiles living in the swamp, so that warnings about real dangerous animals would generalize to the monsters. Much the same applies to ghosts, which are normally not considered in the abstract but described as a person who used to stand in a particular kinship relation; the resemblances between the ghosts and the living are stressed, so that generalization can again occur.

It must be clearly understood, of course, that the sharp division between realistic and unrealistic dangers exists only in the mind of the anthropological observer, and not in that of the Kwoma themselves. In view of this, one might well question whether Whiting's scheme has really much explanatory value, and whether he is saying more than that both realistic dangers and the fear of supernatural ones are learnt from the teachers. As Whiting himself shows, non-observance of warnings about supernatural dangers also has consequences which tend to reinforce the warnings. One of these is simply social disapproval or punishment, the other is, as it were, self-inflicted by the suitable interpretation of natural events as results of the breaches of prohibitions. In this connexion Whiting tells the following story: a Kwoma had prepared a garden site near the supposed dwelling place of *marsalai*. At night there was a bad storm (these occur frequently) and this was believed by the man himself and his friends to be a sign that the monster had been angered by the disturbance. Thus it would seem that what calls for an explanation is the difference in the way Kwoma categorize their worlds, for given this the rest follows.

It is only fair to explain that this was a very early study of Whiting's and one of the very few attempting to trace in detail the process whereby superstitious beliefs and practices are transmitted from one generation to the next. Subsequently he pioneered an entirely fresh approach to the study of the origins of superstition which, while still retaining in its theoretical rationale the language of conditioning, departed from it considerably in practice. One work dealt with the childhood antecedents of the fear of witchcraft and sorcery,[11] but one of his more recent writings will serve to illustrate the method. The particular problem to be singled out for discussion is the fear of ghosts at funeral ceremonies.[12] For the purposes of this exposition, Whiting's arguments will have to be greatly simplified. He starts off with the general problem of social control, suggesting that neither positive reinforcements alone, nor in combination with negative ones, could maintain a complex social system. In other words, he thinks that rewards are insufficient to ensure regular good behaviour, and the inhibitions set up by punishment will usually become rapidly extinct. Other more subtle mechanisms are required, one of the major ones being the fear of supernatural sanctions; there cannot always be an actual policeman present, but the fear of evil acts being punished by ghosts transcends this limitation. Whiting also put forward reasons why the dreaded ghosts are likely to be in the main those of one's parents. On this basis, a specific question was asked, and a hypothesis formulated; these are best expressed in Whiting's own words:

What are the child-rearing conditions that should lead to a preoccupation with parental ghosts? . . . if a parent in caring for a child and satisfying his needs was frequently absent when he was in a state of high need – that is, hungry, cold, or suffering from some other discomfort – he would be very likely to engage in fantasies which would represent his mother or other caretaker satisfying his needs. Assuming that the mother eventually comes and feeds him or covers him up, this act should reinforce his magical thinking and increase the probability that he will produce fantasy images of his mother when she is absent and he is in need. It is our hypothesis that this type of magical thinking underlies a preoccupation with ghosts and spirits . . .[13]

It follows from this that in societies where someone is always around and prepared to gratify a child's need immediately, fear of ghosts ought to be low; and where the child is often left in some distress for a while, it ought to be high. Now it is one thing to formulate a hypothesis, and another to test it with a certain amount of rigour; it is a weakness of much Freudian and even more Jungian psychology that a multitude of interesting hypotheses are generated without being subjected to adequate testing. Whiting, however, did go to great pains to obtain data about both child-rearing conditions and fear of ghosts in more than forty societies, and was able to demonstrate a relationship substantial enough to make it unlikely that it was merely due to chance; on the other hand the fit was far from perfect, so that other factors clearly played a part.

This method appears to hold out the promise of new insights into the child-rearing conditions which tend to produce particular kinds of beliefs. It is necessary, however, to mention one serious limitation: in trying to obtain details of many societies all over the world, one has to rely on ethnographic material of varying quality, some of it old and somewhat unreliable. For instance, it has been shown in relation to witchcraft that the longer the ethnographer stayed in the field, and the more familiar he was with the indigenous language, the more likely it was that he would report the presence of witchcraft beliefs.[14] Fortunately most modern anthropological reports do not suffer from such shortcomings, and we now turn to the different perspective they offer.

REFERENCES

1 B. F. Skinner, *Science and Human Behavior*, New York: Macmillan, 1953, p. 65.
2 B. F. Skinner, *Walden Two*, New York: Macmillan, 1948, p. 101.
3 *Journal of Experimental Psychology*, 1948, 38, pp. 168–72.
4 *Science and Human Behavior*, p. 85.
5 *op. cit.*, p. 86.

6 *op. cit.*, pp. 350–51.

7 *op. cit.*, p. 70.

8 A. Charles Catania and David Cutts, 'Experimental control of superstitious responding in humans', *Journal of Experimental Analysis of Behavior*, 1963, 6, pp. 203–8.

9 *Science and Human Behavior*, p. 351.

10 *Becoming a Kwoma*, New Haven: Yale University Press, 1941.

11 J. W. M. Whiting and I. L. Child, *Child Training and Personality: A cross-cultural study*, New Haven: Yale University Press, 1953.

12 J. W. M. Whiting, 'Sorcery, Sin and the Superego', in M. R. Jones (ed.), *Nebraska Symposium on Motivation*, Lincoln, Neb.: University of Nebraska Press, 1959.

13 *op. cit.*, p. 182.

14 Raul Naroll, *Data Quality Control*, New York: The Free Press of Glencoe, 1962, p. 153.

CHAPTER SIX

Superstition as a Social Phenomenon

... in the diocese of Constance, twenty-eight German miles from the town of Ratisbon in the direction of Salzburg, a violent hailstorm destroyed all the fruit, crops and vineyards in a belt one mile wide, so that the vines hardly bore fruit for three years. This was brought to the notice of the Inquisition, since the people clamoured for an enquiry to be held; many beside all the townsmen being of the opinion that it was caused by witchcraft ...

And it is known that these women have entered into an open pact with the devil, because they revealed secret matters to those who come to them to be cured. For they suddenly disclose to such a person the cause of his calamity, telling him that he has been bewitched either in his own person or in his possessions because of some quarrel he has had with a neighbour or with some other woman or man ...

Malleus Maleficarum (fifteenth-century Europe)

While the preceding chapters have in the main concentrated on the psychological aspects of superstition, social factors have unavoidably and repeatedly obtruded themselves. Thus it has been shown that Skinner's account tacitly assumes some of the things it tries to explain, by underplaying the role of social transmission. The origins of most superstitions are shrouded in the mists of time, and admit nothing more than unverifiable speculation. On the other hand, new collective superstitions do occasionally arise and thus provide an opportunity for studying their genesis.

One of these was the so-called Vailala madness, which emerged in Papua around 1919, one of a series of 'cargo cults' in Melanesia. This has a variety of manifestations, some of which were grossly physical. Large numbers of people were affected by some sort of giddiness, reeling around without proper muscular control. An eye-witness account describes these bizarre scenes:

the natives . . . were taking a few quick steps in front of them, and would then stand, jabber and gesticulate, at the same time swaying the head from side to side; also bending the body from side to side from the hips, the legs appearing to be held firm. Others would take quick steps forward and stop, placing the hands on the hips, jabbering continuously, swaying the head from side to side, and moving the trunk of the body backwards and forwards, remaining in this position for approximately a minute . . .[1]

The possession was accompanied by peculiar sensations in the stomach, and some of the leaders in such a state burst into unintelligible utterances said to be 'Djaman' (German). Their main teaching was that traditional customs and ceremonies should be abolished. They inveighed against such evils as adultery and theft, and large poles were brought into use for divinatory purposes. Carried by several bearers, they were alleged to move under their own power and seek out evil-doers; the pole would take them to the dwelling of the guilty person, who was thereby led to confess.[2] The most important body of doctrine, however, was the prophecy of the coming of a steamer with the spirits of the dead ancestors on board. They would bring with them the 'Cargo', lots of trading goods to be distributed to the villagers. The ancestors (who by a curious quirk were sometimes conceived as white) would restore all trade to its rightful owners, the Papuans, and get rid of the whites. The leaders claimed to be in constant touch with the spirits through messages that fell down from the sky, or were received in mystical manner through flagpoles. This by no means exhausts the colourful features of this movement, but will be sufficient to convey the general flavour. Incidentally, it is interesting to note that some twelve years later it had turned into a living legend, with people believing that the vessel had in fact called.

Contemporary accounts of the movement fastened upon its spectacular possession elements, attempting to account for it

× all of which applies on a sophisticated
philosophical level as well as of
Koestler on Platos forms

mostly in psychological terms. It was said to be a 'mass hysteria', pathological in nature and indicative of character weakness, suggestibility and credulity. Whilst some of this is probably true, it does not really help us to understand the nature of these eccentric superstitions, their particular content and why they arose at that specific point in time.

The Vailala madness and similar movements have recently been re-examined by a sociologist, Peter Worsley,[3] in relation to their social and cultural background. For Worsley the key to their genesis is the rapid social change introduced by Europeans, which disoriented the indigenous population. The old values and beliefs were undermined, and new goals presented, especially in terms of a richer material life. In the absence of any adequate means to achieve these new goals, profound tensions arose which on the one hand overflowed into the hysterical behaviour described, and on the other achieved a fantasy outlet in the shape of the cargo that was prophesied. This broad interpretation is supported by Worsley with a good deal of specific detail; for instance, as one would expect, the most active members of the movements were not those still living in a predominantly traditional situation, but people subjected to mission influence or those who had worked as indentured labourers on plantations.

The general thesis that social movements, many of them characterized by grossly superstitious sets of beliefs, arise from people's unsatisfied needs has been put forward by Hans Toch.[4] He puts it as follows: 'Miracles provide prospects of change in situations that are objectively hopeless, and offer comfort and a basis for enduring situations that are objectively intolerable.' While Toch was not primarily concerned with superstitions, but social movements of all kinds, many of his illustrations are relevant. One might also mention for instance the multiplicity of syncretistic sects flourishing among Africans in the Union of South Africa, where political action is not at present a practicable outlet for their grievances. One broad generalization suggested is that stressful social situations are favourable to the emergence and acceptance of superstitious beliefs. Unfortunately it would be very difficult to prove this in any rigorous manner. One would first of all need operational definitions for the two concepts of 'superstition' and 'stress'; given these, one would look at the extent to which the two go together in as large as possible a variety of human societies. The trouble is that 'superstition' is hard to define in this way, as has already been explained at length; and the position is not much easier as regards 'stress'. One can be sure that both are present in some degree everywhere, but the task of assessing any quantitative relationships between two such diffuse phenomena seems a hopeless one.

Is there nothing that can be done then? The answer is that it is possible to focus on more specific aspects of superstitious behaviour, such as spirit possession, which is a clear-cut pattern of behaviour, extremely widespread in space and time. In ancient Greece, the worshippers of Dionysius worked themselves up into a frenzy. With 'foaming lips and eyes that rolled wildly, and reckless madness-clouded soul' they became possessed by the bull-god. With complete abandon they threw themselves upon a young bull, tore it to pieces with their bare hands and ate the raw, steaming flesh. In twentieth-century Europe, in a more subdued key, one finds the medium in the dim seance room possessed by the spirits of the departed; and basically similar performances are enacted all over the world. For a long time, not surprisingly, it was the sensational aspects of the trance state on which attention was focussed; and no doubt it is in itself a most interesting psychological phenomenon. Of late, however, concern has shifted to the problem that primarily concerns us here, namely the social type of person who comes to be selected, if one may put it that way, as a medium by the spirits. For the brief account which follows I am largely indebted to the brilliant Malinowski Lecture by I. M. Lewis.[5] Starting with observations based on his own fieldwork among the Somali, he was impressed by the fact that possession looked as though it were one of the weapons in the sex war. Thereupon he went on to collect numerous other instances from ethnographic reports relating to other areas, and the data seemed to fit in with this notion. One of his examples is from East Africa, where there exist capricious spirits of a particular kind:

They are not worshipped, but frequently plague Kamba women who must then be exorcised. As with possession elsewhere, these afflicted women speak 'with tongues' in an obscure jargon – but despite the problems of communication, their demands are quite clear. What they seek is gifts and attention from their menfolk, usually husbands, each spirit asking for things appropriate to its provenance. Thus Swahili spirits demand embroidered Arab hats, and European spirits articles of European origin. Women make use of the cult to force their husbands to buy new skirts for them.

There is a suggestion here that women are apt to exploit such beliefs deliberately, and indeed Lewis quotes some specific cases of this sort. It would be wrong to imagine, however, that something like a female conspiracy to batten on male gullibility is involved. There is a continuum ranging from utter conviction via half-belief to frank scepticism; but the scepticism usually relates to a particular instance and the existence of the spirits as such is usually not in question. At any rate, Lewis proposes that spirit possession is often a means whereby 'women and other depressed categories exert mystical pressures upon their superiors in circumstances of deprivation and frustration when few other sanctions are available to them'.

It is thus possible to examine the social setting of certain types of superstition, and thereby gain an understanding of the fact that they are not just arbitrary in nature, but sometimes serve certain well-defined purposes. Whilst this idea is novel as regards the phenomena of spirit possession, it has long been applied to witchcraft and sorcery, following the pioneering studies of Evans-Pritchard among the Nuer, and Kluckhohn among the Navaho. Anthropologists draw a distinction between witchcraft and sorcery. Witchcraft is the alleged power of a person to do evil and harm others. The precise details of the notion vary, but it is generally regarded, by the believers, as a psychic attribute of the personality. The power may or may not be under the person's voluntary control, and in the latter case he or she might not even be aware of the evil done. At any rate, witchcraft does not involve any observable physical (including verbal) act on the part of the person. In sorcery, by contrast, there is always the intention to do harm, and this purpose is served by carrying out one of a variety of different acts such as reciting a magical formula or performing some ritual. In other words, while it would be in principle impossible to observe witchcraft at work, one might see sorcery being enacted. Although the conceptual distinction made by anthropologists is clear-cut, this is not necessarily true of the people in many societies where both witchcraft and sorcery supposedly flourish. Since it is not essential to our argument, the same applies to the discussion which follows.

It is widely held by anthropologists that the vicissitudes of human fate are at the root of witchcraft and sorcery beliefs. Misfortunes like illness, accident and death are even more common in pre-literate societies than they are with us; some people thrive and do exceptionally well, while others are wretchedly poor, with barely enough for subsistence. Why is that, and what can one do about it? An answer to both these questions is that witches and sorcerers cause the evil, and one can try and protect oneself by taking counter-measures. It is hard for an educated Westerner to grasp the extent to which such ideas enter into the texture of everyday life. An extract from an autobiography collected by Edward H. Winter[6] from a Bwamba woman in Uganda will help to convey this.

[my mother] gave birth to another child, a son named Isoba. When he was beginning to crawl, he was killed, and the woman who was responsible for his death was killed in turn. They tied her hands and dropped her in the river. That is how they used to treat witches ... my mother ... became pregnant again and bore a girl called Monodani. Six days after she had been born, she died. With the death of that child the people of my father's lineage said, 'We were wrong to suspect that other woman. It must be a spirit who is killing these children.'

A native doctor was consulted, who performed a suitable ritual to protect the mother from that spirit and ensure that future children would survive; but it was not to be.

Then my mother was killed by a man who was jealous of her. He said: 'Why did you marry that old man?'

That man followed her when she was going to fetch some water. She refused to sleep with him, so she was killed by a disease which came from the water. It stripped off her bark-cloth and she went home naked. As soon as she had come out of the water, she fell and became sick. My father was very angry and said to the man: 'Although you have bewitched my wife, you won't eat her' [i.e. die and acquire her spirit].

In spite of the fact that he took her to hospital, she died.

A good deal can be learned about the nature of such beliefs even from this brief fragment. There is the background of high infant mortality, for which evil-doers are supposed to be responsible. When the deaths continued after the witch had been executed, people were quite ready to exonerate her posthumously and lay the blame on another supernatural agency. The subsequent death of the mother herself was attributed to a man. Why this particular man? She had refused him her favours, so he had a grudge against her and thus had a motive for bewitching her. This is very characteristic of the way in which accusations of witchcraft and sorcery originate. A misfortune strikes, and one looks around for some *one* who caused it. Paul Bohannan[7] cast this in the form of a syllogism:

Major premise: Illness is spread by witches.
Minor premise: Illness is spreading.
Conclusion: Witches are present.

The question then becomes 'Who are they?'; sometimes the answer is obvious to the people concerned, and they make an accusation; in other cases recourse is had to diviners and oracles. Whatever the method, the outcome is that the finger is pointed at particular individuals. These are confronted with the 'evidence', and here the reactions vary. In some societies, like the Azande studied by Evans-Pritchard, the accused almost invariably either claim that they are innocent, or at least deny that they have wrought the evil intentionally, and ceremonially take back any malice they may unwittingly have directed at the victim; thus the path to recovery is opened, and treatment can become effective. Alternatively, in other cultures, it is not uncommon for the witch to confess and withdraw her evil power, often undergoing a cleansing ceremony (prior to colonial rule witches were often killed, or at least expelled from the community). An example of the acceptance of the accusation comes from another Bwamba autobiography:

I have tried to marry women, but one of my father's wives made some medicine and bewitched me so that I was unable to marry women. I told my father, 'One of your wives has bewitched me so that I may not marry women.'

My father asked, 'Are you sure? Can you tell me which one?'

93

I said, 'Yes'. I pointed out the wife to my father, and the woman cried for about three days.

Later when I was alone in my house that woman came and said to me, 'You told your father that I have bewitched you so that you may not marry women. Now I ask you to go and bring the woman whom you want to marry.'

That night I went to the woman whom I loved and brought her to my home. After that I married as many other women as I wished.

The background of this particular episode is not known, but one may venture the guess that the man had previously been in some conflict with that wife of his father's, and perhaps she may have impugned his virility in the course of the quarrel. Believing himself to be bewitched, impotence may well have been the result. Certainly in some cases that I investigated myself, this kind of process seems to have been at work. The usual pattern is that a man takes another wife against what he knows to be the wishes of the first one, who utters threats; the husband becomes convinced that witchcraft or sorcery have been used, and proves impotent with the new wife. This is the kind of 'self-fulfilling prophecy' whereby witchcraft and sorcery beliefs are causally effective in bringing about that which is most feared.

The main point to note, however, is that accusations are not haphazardly directed at anyone, nor is it mysterious strangers who form the main target. On the contrary, it is people with whom one has experienced close social relationships, that have gone wrong in some way.

There is now a great deal of systematic evidence for the regularity and lawfulness of such patterns. One of the most precise and quantitative studies in this sphere is that of M. G. Marwick,[3] who presented several detailed breakdowns, one of which is shown below in condensed form.

| | *Accuser and Sorcerer* | |
	Related	Unrelated, or Relationship not known
Accusation linked with quarrel	52	27
No indication of such a link	18	4

From this table two kinds of information can be derived about the Cewa of Northern Rhodesia (now Zambia). Looking at the columns, it can be seen that about 70 per cent of all accusations were directed against people known to be related to the accuser; the rows indicate that four out of five of the accusations were preceded by a quarrel. Since many of the accusations are the outcome of consulting a diviner, it might seem puzzling at first sight how such regularity comes about; but there is really little mystery here. In the first place, diviners are usually shrewd observers of social affairs in their area; they know the friendship and kinship patterns, and keep a close watch on jealousies and troubles of all kinds. Some diviners with whom I discussed the matter prided themselves on having built up what amounts to a highly efficient intelligence service. The *modus operandi* of diviners ensures that their store of information can be utilized in the course of the seance. If, perchance, his knowledge of the situation is insufficient, he can always tell his clients to come back later; with Cewa diviners, this is in fact the rule.

It may be of interest to describe the procedure among the Konkomba of Northern Ghana,[9] which illustrates the basic principles involved. Divination takes place in two stages. At first, the diviner reads a message from cowrie shells which is cast in the nebulous general terms familiar to us from the seaside fortune-teller. The second stage is conceived as a test of the diviner's first reading. The person or persons who are seeking aid and advice decide in the absence of the diviner himself on three questions of the 'Twenty Questions' type, e.g. 'Does he live in village X?' Three sticks are laid on the ground, each representing one of the questions. The diviner then points with his staff to one of the sticks, and the one touched is the one where the answer is affirmative. Thus the original vague accusations are gradually narrowed down to particular individuals. So far it looks as though the diviner were really functioning in a paranormal fashion, and this is undoubtedly how it seems to his clients. However, as in a conjuring trick, there are a few vital details to be filled in. Thus although the diviner is absent while the questions are being formulated, his assistant remains present; moreover, when the staff is being manipulated the assistant holds one end of it, thereby being in a position to provide cues as to which of the sticks is to be touched. Hence, in Tait's words, these operations 'in fact reveal the suspicions, conscious or unconscious, of those who consult the diviner'.

The diviner's function is of course not confined to pin-pointing a guilty party. He is consulted in the main when people are faced with difficulties and misfortunes, and is expected not only to pronounce on the causes, but also to provide remedies. These consist in suggesting sacrifices and other procedures to restore ritual purity, or in advising people to abstain from sinful acts which led to the unfortunate events. Thus if a witch is uncovered and has confessed he or she may undergo a ritual of cleansing; if the omission of a sacrifice to the ancestors has caused illness, it can be repaired and atoned for; a convicted sorcerer may be punished; and in all these different ways harmony in the community is restored. As Tait put it:

The diviner's role is to point out ritual and moral omissions. He recalls his society to religious and moral duty and by his insistence on avoidance or expiation of offences he releases his fellows from the burden of guilt and gives them security.

The diviner forms part of a wider system of beliefs in witchcraft and sorcery, which has moral implications. If you behave unpleasantly to your neighbour, you risk his revenge through witchcraft or sorcery; on the other hand, if you are envious of someone and your envy or hostility is shown without restraint then you yourself may be suspected of sorcery or witchcraft. Marwick cites many cases where a misfortune is interpreted by others as the result of a transgression:

Mkanjo went to work in a mine in Southern Rhodesia, taking his wife with him. One day, as he was operating a pneumatic drill, a loose piece of rock came away and killed him. His wife argued that his death was the result of the hatred of the African foreman who, she said, must have deliberately marked the position of the hole on a loose piece of rock. Mkanjo's relatives refused to believe this, saying that his wife must have committed adultery and thus broken the strict sexual taboo imposed on the wives of all those engaged in dangerous or delicate operations, such as mining, iron smelting and *kacaso* distilling. (p. 228.)

The general thesis pioneered by Evans-Pritchard, and later extensively documented in a variety of societies, is that beliefs which naïve Europeans view as crude superstition are not just odd and useless excrescences, mere aberrations of the human spirit. On the contrary, they emerge as indicators of social conflicts and tensions, since the occurrence of misfortunes is linked to frictions among people; and also as a framework within which tensions and hostilities may be reduced, since there are prescribed ways of handling social relationships disturbed in this manner, and specialists such as diviners whose function it is to act as mediators.

It is important to note that these broad social implications of witchcraft, sorcery and other beliefs could never have been discovered by the study of individuals as such. They emerged only from an examination of the ways in which these beliefs functioned within a context of social relationships, and for this purpose the psychological approach has to be supplemented by the anthropological and sociological ones. Nonetheless, the ways in which people in such societies conceive of the world around them differ in some fundamental respects from those of the standard educated European. It will be necessary to scrutinize such differences more closely, and this leads back to the psychological processes of individuals who are, after all, the carriers of cultural norms.

REFERENCES

1 Quoted in Peter Worsley, *The Trumpet Shall Sound*, MacGibbon & Kee, 1957.
2 Similar beliefs existed in various other parts of the world. For instance the Ashanti used to have a custom of 'carrying the corpse', and the dead body was said to lead the bearers to the witch responsible for his death. cf. R. S. Rattray, *Religion and Art in Ashanti*, Oxford University Press, 1927.
3 *op. cit.*
4 *The Social Psychology of Social Movements*, Methuen, 1966, p. 43.
5 'Spirit Possession and Deprivation Cults', *Man*, 1966, 1, pp. 307–29.
6 *Beyond the Mountains of the Moon*, Kegan Paul, 1959, pp. 110–11.
7 *Social Anthropology*, New York: Holt Rinehart, 1963.
8 *Sorcery in its Social Setting*, Manchester University Press, 1965. Based on Table XXVI, p. 217.
9 David Tait, *The Konkomba of Northern Ghana*, Oxford University Press, 1961.

CHAPTER SEVEN

Superstition as a Mode of Thinking

We are too hasty when we set down our ancestors in the gross for fools, for the monstrous inconsistencies (as they seem to us) involved in their creed of witchcraft. In the relations of this visible world we find them to have been as rational, and shrewd to detect an historic anomaly, as ourselves. But when once the invisible world was supposed to be opened, and the lawless agency of bad spirits assumed, what measures of probability, of decency, of fitness, or proportion – of that which distinguishes the likely from the palpably absurd – could they have to guide them in the rejection or admission of any particular testimony? – that maidens pined away, wasting inwardly as their waxen images consumed before a fire – that corn was lodged, and cattle lamed – that whirlwinds uptore in diabolic revelry the oaks of the forest – or that spits and kettles only danced a fearful-innocent vagary about some rustic's kitchen when no wind was stirring – were all equally probable when no law of agency was understood.

Charles Lamb *The Essays of Elia*

The problem of 'primitive thought' has long held a fascination for students of man, and numerous volumes have been written on it. Until the present century, most of these writers based their theories at best on second-hand reports of ethnographers, and at worst on the tales of travellers who brought back stories about the fantastic ideas entertained by strange and remote peoples. Of the two outstanding men in the early years of English anthropology, Sir Edward Burnett Tylor had at least travelled to the

New World. Sir James Frazer, on the other hand, produced his monumental work without venturing far afield. Beattie[1] quotes a report that he 'when asked if he had ever seen one of the primitive people about whose customs he had written so many volumes, tersely replied "God forbid!"'. It is all the more remarkable what they were able to achieve, especially Tylor, many of whose ideas have stood the test of time. However, as regards magic and other superstitions, both their approaches were, as Evans-Pritchard termed it, intellectualist. Tylor examined, for instance, the beliefs in spiritual beings and personal spirits pervading nature which he called 'animism'. In accounting for its origin, Tylor put forward the view that primitive man thought about his experiences in dreams, visions and trance states, disease and death, and tried to make sense of them by postulating a soul which is the spiritual counterpart of the body, extending this notion to other animate beings and also the inanimate world. With regard to magic, Tylor considered it the result of a confusion on the part of the savage between analogy and causality. This topic has already been touched upon earlier, but an example will serve as a reminder. Among the Ga in Ghana it was common practice for a husband who went on a journey to give some medicine to his wife or wives; the main ingredient was a plant which closes up firmly on being touched. The analogy involved in this protection against adultery is obvious. Tylor treated this kind of thing as a logical error and called it a 'delusion'. At the same time, he was the first to raise the question how it was possible that such delusions persisted, and the answers he suggested are still the best available. They are, briefly, as follows: magic is often a counterpart of everyday life activities, whereby human action brings about the desired results (e.g. garden magic); magic is often supposed to bring about natural events, which occur anyway (e.g. rain making); failure is attributed either to imperfect performance of the necessary rites and spells, or to more powerful hostile counter-magic; in any case, it is not always clear what is to be reckoned as failure, and a small proportion of successes may be quite sufficient to reinforce (as Skinner would term it) the beliefs. Tylor even mentioned the psychological effects of magic, which are often real enough: 'Prophecy tends to fulfil itself, as where the magician, by putting into a victim's mind the belief that fatal arts have been practised against him, can slay him with this idea as with a material weapon.'[2] With regard to the example given earlier, the husband takes care to ensure that his wife, and perhaps also potential lovers, know that preventive magical medicine has been administered, and this is likely to act as a deterrent.

Frazer, whose theories discussed before are also germane to the present chapter, took over some of Tylor's central ideas. He elaborated them, and cast them into a more rigid form, thereby rendering them less valid. Thus he transformed the modes of thinking described by Tylor into 'laws', claiming that 'savages' implicitly believed and applied these. In this way he introduced a categorical distinction between the thinking of 'savages' and 'civilized' which Tylor does not appear to have intended. There is no doubt, however, that both interpreted superstition as errors of logical thinking. Influenced by the rationalistic temper of their time, they conceived of 'savages' as essentially reasonable people who sought after the truth but failed to reach it.

This basic assumption of the 'English School', as it was then called, came to be challenged by a prominent disciple of the French sociologist Durkheim, Lévy-Bruhl. The title of his best-known book, *How Natives Think*,[3] is a somewhat unhappy translation of the French title *Les Fonctions Mentales dans les Sociétés Inférieures*. He reproached Tylor and Frazer for the fact that they took it for granted that the mental functioning of primitive people was identical to our own, and were thereby prevented from considering alternative hypotheses. His own work consisted very largely of a juxtaposition, with a wealth of illustrative detail, of civilized and primitive modes of thinking. The outcome suggested to him a qualitative difference: while civilized thought is rational, logical and scientific, primitive thought is affective, poetic and mythical. Lévy-Bruhl attached a pair of labels to the modes of thinking, calling them 'logical' and 'pre-logical' respectively. These have led to endless misunderstanding of his position, since 'pre-logical' was widely interpreted as meaning 'illogical' or even stupid and innately inferior. A certain ambiguity in his writing accounts for this kind of misunderstanding, though it is certainly not what he meant to convey. Two passages will make this clear:

As the social environment where they live is different from ours, and precisely because it is different, the external world which they perceive differs also from that which we perceive. No doubt they have the senses... and the same cerebral structure. But one must take into account what the collective representations* contribute to each of their perceptions. Whatever the object with which they are faced, it has mystical properties attached to it which are inseparable, and the mind of primitive man does not in fact separate when he perceives it.

In this way, the exigencies of logical thought are elicited, established and then strengthened in each individual mind by the uninterrupted pressure of the social milieu, by means of language itself and through what is transmitted in the forms of language. This constitutes a heritage of which no one is deprived in our society, and which no one can even have the thought of rejecting . . .

Quite other are the conditions where the pre-logical mentality obtains. No doubt it is also socially transmitted, through the intermediary of language and of concepts without which it could not find expression . . . But these concepts differ from ours and, consequently, the mental operations differ also.

What Lévy-Bruhl was saying is that primitive and civilized men have the same biological characteristics, but owing to the divergent social influences impinging upon them, their outlook on the world is vastly different. One of Levy-Bruhl's major contributions is the avoidance of the confusion implicit in Tylor's and Frazer's account between the process of thinking and its content. They had written as if they had a special window into the 'savage's' mind, observing it at work, when in fact they were dealing merely with the nature of the content, and that often filtered through sources of doubtful reliability. Moreover, although he perhaps placed insufficient stress on this, Lévy-Bruhl definitely recognized that what he called pre-logical modes of thinking persist side by side with logical ones in civilized societies.

When anthropologists began to live among pre-literate peoples, acquiring their language and sharing their everyday activities, it became increasingly evident that the allegedly sharp contrast between their and our own mode of thinking was at least in part

*More or less what we to-day would call 'culture'.

an illusion created by those who looked at them from a distance. While there is often a gap, it is not an unbridgeable one. Thus Evans-Pritchard relates how odd the curious explanations of misfortunes given by the Azande appeared to him at first, when from our Western point of view these had obvious natural causes. Then he went on: 'but after a while I learnt the idiom of their thought and applied notions of witchcraft as spontaneously as themselves in situations where the concept was relevant'.[4]

Although unfamiliar, the idiom is far from being totally alien to us, probably for two main reasons. The first is that much of our thought in certain spheres, particularly the religious, poetic and artistic, moves along rather similar lines. The second, logically prior, reason is that all of us pass in infancy and childhood through a period of mental development characterized by many features of magic and animism. In saying this one must guard against the risk of suspicion that one is perpetuating the hoary myth which equates primitive adults with civilized children. On the contrary, the point is that children in all societies, at whatever level of technology, have certain stages in common. There is now a great deal of evidence to support such a view, due mainly to the epoch-making studies of the Swiss psychologist Jean Piaget, who will probably rank with Freud and Pavlov as one of the giants. For nearly half a century he, together with an increasing number of followers, charted the development of thinking in the child. He showed that until about the age of ten or eleven, children's concepts of such basic categories as space, matter, time and causality differ fundamentally from those of normal adults. He discovered this by means of a large number of highly ingenious though often basically simple experiments. For instance, to take a well-known example, adults take it for granted that if a piece of matter assumes another shape, its quantity is not altered thereby. In order to investigate whether this principle of conservation is understood by small children, Piaget presented them with two balls of plasticine which the children agreed were equal in amount. He then rolled one of them into a sausage, whereupon children up to the age of about seven or eight thought that the amount of plasticine in the sausage had become smaller.

While the experiments are often simple, the theoretical

formulation of Piaget's more recent work is cast in a highly sophisticated logico-mathematical framework which need not concern us here.[5] In some of his earlier studies, which relied more on verbal questioning than experiment, Piaget took a considerable interest in the magical and animistic aspects of children's thinking.[6] He started from the position, reached on the basis of prior research, that the young child is incapable of distinguishing clearly between his self and the outside world; moreover, the child at that early stage cannot differentiate between psychological and physical phenomena. It follows that the child is totally egocentric, not of course in the sense of 'selfish', but in the sense that he is quite incapable of even conceiving of a perspective differing from his own. The child's thoughts, feelings and wishes are mixed up with what we would call the external reality to which they relate. Thus psychological processes are objectified, and things endowed with psychological attributes. Dreams seem to come from the outside, words are indissolubly linked with the objects to which they refer, and speaking is felt to be a way of acting upon things. Conversely, the physical world is not sharply divided off as material and inanimate, but on the contrary regarded as though it were possessed of life, consciousness and will.

In many ways it is a stranger universe than that of Alice through the looking-glass, since Alice after all retained her sense of personal identity, judging her grotesque environment in terms of this standard. The world of the very young child probably has some of the attributes of the looking-glass world, but the child beholding it would find nothing surprising in the tiger-lily talking and the leg of mutton sitting in the chair. For an adult it is all very peculiar, and yet in some ways oddly familiar, because we have all been through such a stage, though most of us cannot remember it except in snatches; and therein perhaps lies the attraction such works of art retain for grown-ups. It may well be, indeed, that creative artists and writers remain in touch with this early and more undifferentiated mode of awareness more closely than the rest of us. Certainly one of the most striking accounts of spontaneous child magic is contained in the autobiographical *Father and Son* by Edmund Gosse, which Piaget quotes. Nothing in Gosse's early environment, with its oppressive restrictions and arid religiosity, provided him with any models of magical ideas or practices to imitate; and yet he managed at the age of about five or six to evolve his own.

Being as restricted, then, and yet as active my mind took refuge in an infantile species of natural magic. This contended with the definite ideas of religion which my parents were continuing, with too mechanical a persistency, to force into my nature and it ran parallel with them. I formed strange superstitions, which I can only render intelligible by naming some concrete examples. I persuaded myself that if I could only discover the proper words to say or the proper passes to make, I could induce the gorgeous birds and butterflies in my Father's illustrated manuals to come to life and fly out of the book, leaving holes behind them. I believed, that, when at the Chapel, we sang, drearily and slowly, loud hymns of experience and humiliation, I could boom forth with a sound equal to that of dozens of the singers, if I could only hit upon the formula. During morning and evening prayers, which were extremely lengthy and fatiguing, I fancied that one of my two selves could flit up, and sit clinging to the cornice, and look down on my other self and the rest of us, if I could only find the key. I laboured for hours in search of these formulas, thinking to compass my ends by means absolutely irrational. For example, I was convinced that if I could only count consecutive numbers long enough, without losing one, I should suddenly, on reaching some far distant figure, find myself in possession of the great secret. I feel quite sure that nothing external suggested these ideas of magic . . .

All this ferment of mind was entirely unobserved by my parents. But when I formed the belief, that it was necessary for the success of my practical magic, that I should hurt myself, and when, as a matter of fact, I began, in extreme secrecy, to run pins into my flesh and bang my joints with books, no one will be surprised to hear that my Mother's attention was drawn to the fact that I was looking 'delicate'.

Apart from this literary source, Piaget collected a good deal of information about childhood magic; though since this is almost impossible to elicit in practice without prolonged observation,[7] most of his material is derived from recollections of adults. They included numerous rituals to ensure success and ward off danger, or magic due to mystic 'participation' (a term Piaget adopted from Lévy-Bruhl) between objects. A particularly charming instance of the last may be cited:

A little girl of six used to pass often with her governess by a lake where some rare water-lilies grew. Every time she would throw some little stones into the water (always choosing them round and white) and taking care not to be seen by the governess. She thought that the next day water-lilies would appear in the place where the stones had fallen. For this reason, in the hope of thus being able to reach the flowers she always threw the stones quite near the edge.

After reviewing various forms of child magic Piaget offers a penetrating discussion of their origins, relating his own views to those of Frazer and Freud. He shows that Frazer's account remains descriptive rather than explanatory, whilst the Freudian account is more adequate but seems to endow the infant with the intellectual capacities of an adult. Piaget's own theory focusses on the diffuse nature of the cognitive relationship between a child and his environment, as already indicated. In support of his interpretation Piaget further suggests that there are certain situations in adult waking life where the boundary between the person and his environment temporarily loses its sharpness, and under such conditions a recurrence of childish magic is to be expected. Among such conditions are intense anxiety, and an exclusive preoccupation with a particular desire. Piaget then relates a number of examples, such as that of the nervous lecturer who feels compelled to walk to a particular spot in order that the lecture should be a success, or the man impatiently waiting for his wife to finish her cigarette before going out, who caught himself sucking furiously at his pipe to make her finish more quickly.

Before leaving the topic of childhood magic, it should be pointed out that Piaget was not concerned with the rich store of socially transmitted superstitions which form part of the traditions of childhood. Many of these have been recorded in the delightful book by the Opies.[8] Some of these reflect age-old concerns, such as the wish for luck or courage; others indicate more recent needs, as for instance passing examinations. A special section is devoted to the avoidance of lines on pavements; this is often cited as *the* typical superstition, though none of the theories seem to offer any adequate explanation of it, at least on the assumption that it is adopted spontaneously. The chances are that this is a socially learnt superstition, as it has been known a long time – Dr Johnson apparently would not step on lines. The wide prevalence of such beliefs or half-beliefs means that even in our own society children who mix with others tend to be exposed from school age onwards to superstitious ideas, however rationalistic and devoid of fairy tales their home environment may be; hence this factor cannot be altogether neglected.

After the brief digression we return to the second part of Piaget's study, concerned with animism, i.e. the attribution of consciousness to things. This set of notions is capable of being fairly readily elicited by systematic questioning, and Piaget presents a wealth of material, of which only one example can be drawn:

We hung a metal box in front of Vel, in such a way that, on letting go of the box, the string unwound making the box turn round and round. 'Why does it turn?' – *Because the string is twisted.* – 'Why does the string turn too?' – *Because it wants to unwind itself.* – 'Why?' – *Because it wants to be unwound* (=it wants to resume its original position, in which the string was unwound). – 'Does the string know it is twisted?' – *Yes. I am sure.* 'How do you think it knows?' – *Because it feels it is all twisted.*

Piaget, according to his usual practice, distinguishes four stages of animism: 1. all things are conscious, at least potentially; 2. things that can move are conscious; 3. things that can move of their own accord are conscious; 4. consciousness is restricted to animals. Children tend to be in the first stage up to about six or seven, and reach the fourth roughly by eleven or twelve; there are however very wide individual variations. Animism has been studied with children in various parts of the world, and the broad sequence has been generally found to hold.[9] Although the systematic evidence for childhood magic is a good deal weaker, this is probably largely due to the difficulties in securing it. What we do know appears consistent with Piaget's view that following the initial undifferentiated phase of thinking in the child, magic and animism are complementary while the self is not yet fully detached from the external world. The child, for instance, may be under the impression that the sun and moon follow him when he is walking; and this may be either a magical ('I make them move') or animistic ('they follow me') phenomenon, or both may co-exist. Piaget further argues that during the next stage, while the self has become separate from things, thereby eliminating purely magical thinking, there still persists for a while a confusion between subjective and objective, resulting in animism lingering on for a time. It is doubtful whether this case has really been made out, and it certainly does not emerge clearly from the material presented. Apart from these details in the phasing of development, however, Piaget has certainly demonstrated that children pass through stages of magical and animistic thinking, and research in different cultures shows that this is likely to be a universal process.

If we accept the basic similarity in the development of thinking for all normal members of the human species, how can we explain the contrasts between Western industrial and traditional societies? The older view, expressed very sharply by Lévy-Bruhl and still widely accepted in a more attenuated form, is this: in traditional societies the prevailing intellectual atmosphere is magical and mythical. Language, folk-lore and religion all combine to shape the growing mind into a common mould favouring the persistence of what we might broadly call superstition; self and external world, name and thing never come to be sharply separated, so that magico-mystical concepts pervade the mode of thinking throughout life. In Western societies, on the other hand, the predominantly naturalistic and rational ideology counteracts the earlier notions, enforces the differentiation of self from environment and thereby fosters an objective outlook. Now it is not suggested that this older view is altogether wrong, but rather that it over-accentuates the differences between cultures, by exaggerating the rationality of the West and under-estimating that of the traditional societies. Our own categories of thinking have gained in subtlety what they have lost in clear definition since the harshly rationalist days of the last century. The building bricks of our world, which used to be Lord Kelvin's hard billiard balls, have melted into packets of energy; the crisp division into body and mind has given way to the insights of psychosomatic medicine which stresses the interaction between mental and physical processes. As we have learnt more we have become more humble about the worth of our own ideas and values, and more prepared to concede the extent to which our modes of thinking fall short of what remains the ideal of rationality.

This has been skilfully analysed in a recent essay by Robin Horton,[10] who stressed the continuities and resemblances between African traditional or mythological and Western scientific thought. What Horton, like some others before him, regards as the fundamental difference between the two modes of thought is this: in traditional cultures there are no properly formulated alternatives to the traditional body of beliefs, while scientifically sophisticated cultures do have a rich variety of such alternatives available for their members. Since the belief system in traditional cultures is monolithic, people cannot readily move outside it, let alone abandon it. This analysis is certainly convincing as far as societies devoid of contact with the outside world are concerned; but it does not really help us to understand why, in the present situation of intensive culture-contact and rapid social change when alternatives become increasingly available, people should still be so reluctant to abandon their old beliefs. It is likely that Horton's interpretation is itself too rationalistic, in so far as it ignores the importance and persistence of emotional learning during childhood, when traditional beliefs were strongly reinforced.

Another aspect of traditional thought noted by Horton is people's inability to tolerate ignorance, in contrast to the scientist who is ever ready to discard a theory which is found not to work, even when there is no other one to replace it. Related to this in traditional societies is, according to Horton, the limited development of any notion of coincidence. The tendency is always to assign a definite cause to a happening:

When a rotten branch falls off a tree and kills a man walking underneath, there has to be a definite explanation of the calamity. Perhaps the man quarrelled with a half-brother over some matter of inheritance, and the latter worked the fall of the branch through a sorcerer. Or perhaps he misappropriated lineage property, and the lineage ancestors brought the branch down on his head. The idea that the whole thing could have come about through the accidental convergence of two independent chains of events is inconceivable because it is psychologically intolerable. To entertain it would be to admit that the episode was inexplicable and unpredictable: a glaring confession of ignorance. *Our approach is rooted similarly we always suppose a cause — even if we can't locate it.*

Now the notion of 'coincidence' is a crucial one, lying right at the core of our problem, and therefore a good deal of attention must be devoted to it. This is because a given event or phenomenon may be regarded as clear proof of the intervention of occult forces by superstitious people, yet be dismissed as mere coincidence by the enlightened sceptic. Since the event is the same, what differs is the mode of thinking about it and judging it. Are there any firm guides to help us to decide 'objectively' what may be regarded as a coincidence? Let us turn to the lawyers, who have to resolve such issues in practice. Two eminent authorities[11] propose the following formulation:

We speak of coincidences whenever (1) the conjunction of two or more events in certain spatial or temporal relations is very unlikely by ordinary standards and (2) is for some reason significant or important, provided (3) that they occur without human contrivance and (4) are independent of each other.

The example used to illustrate the definition again concerns a tree – it is extraordinary how popular trees are with writers on coincidence. At any rate, the case is one where person A strikes person B, who is stunned by the blow and falls to the ground; thereupon a tree falls down, killing B by crushing him. This conforms to the definition of being (1) a rare combination of events, (2) important because they resulted in a death, (3) not deliberately brought about by A, and (4) the blow and the falling of the tree were independent of each other. In connexion with the last point Hart and Honoré state that if B had fallen against the tree with sufficient force to bring it down, this would not have been a coincidence, and in this case A would have been the cause of B's death since there was an unbroken chain of causation. Here we come up at once against the slipperiness of the concept, since it is possible to hold another view. It seems plausible to argue that the brittleness of a large tree (unless A had a prior knowledge of this) such that the impact of a human body would fell it is such an unlikely phenomenon as to constitute a coincidence. Perhaps another example will make this even clearer: suppose A pushes B, who happens to step on a poisonous snake in the grass which rears and bites him, causing his death. Here we have again an unbroken chain of causation of the same type, which would surely qualify as a coincidence.

The authors also point to a fundamental difficulty in making a judgement as to whether or not a particular conjunction of events is or is not to be regarded as a coincidence: 'Just how unlikely must a conjunction be to rank as a coincidence, and in the light of what knowledge is likelihood to be assessed?' And they conclude: 'The only answer is: "very unlikely in the light of the knowledge available to ordinary men".' In admitting this, they have really sold the pass. This is because 'ordinary men' will vary widely in their judgements of probability, depending on their prior experiences, beliefs and values. One man dreams about an air crash and, reading an account of one the following morning, believes that he has the gift of prophecy; another who has a similar experience dismisses it as 'mere coincidence'.

In the 1930s a prominent German writer published a book entitled *Chance and Fate*,[12] which went through many editions and was also issued as a paperback. The major part of this book consists of a large collection of extraordinary coincidences. I shall quote the first one, typical of the rest:

In the night from 7th to 8th February 1934 a violent storm arose over Berlin, toppling some large masts onto the monument of Henry the Child in the Siegesallee, which was badly damaged. Particularly the right-hand one ... of a series of busts ... originally modelled after the head of Henri Zille who was a friend of the sculptor, was hit and thrown from its base. During the morning following that night the creator of this marble group, Professor August Kraus, died of a heart attack in his house in Grunewald; and in his garden the sudden gust had at the same time also thrown a bust from its base. (p. 9.)

There are those of us who would respond to this kind of thing with a deprecatory 'so what!'. But Scholz piles up one fantastic coincidence after the other: the fragments of ancient Greek vases coming together in the most unlikely manner; the two cases of malaria arriving simultaneously in a clinic where there had not been any for years; a woman losing an exposed roll of film and when buying another one two years later it turned out to be the one lost previously; a candidate for an examination opening his book at random to study, and lo and behold it was the text on which he was later to be questioned; and so on, and so forth. For Scholz, it was altogether too much to dismiss all these events as matters of chance; and so he developed some notions which hardly deserve the title of a theory, but may perhaps be called a series of *ad hoc* principles. For instance, lost objects have a miraculous habit of finding their way back to the original owner, like the exposed film; so there must be a 'force of attraction' between an object and its owner which influences third parties, triggering off in them behaviour that leads to the coming together of object and owner. There is also a force of attraction governing sounds, names, words and numbers; for instance, in a lottery the three winning numbers were 777, 77, and 7; and one person had all these tickets! It cannot just be chance – it must be the design of fate.

The whole book displays the mystical and poetic (the writer was of course a *littérateur*) qualities Lévy-Bruhl attributed to the primitive mentality. Note that Scholz was not treated as a crank, isolated and ignored; the book received extensive notice in the press and periodicals, was discussed on the wireless, and seems to have convinced large numbers of twentieth-century civilized Westerners. So the gap between modern and primitive thought is much narrower than many of us fondly imagine. This, indeed, is the burden of one part of Horton's thesis which led him to end with a warning of the 'trap which the Western layman characteristically falls into – the trap which makes him feel he is keeping up with the scientists when in fact he is no nearer to them than the African peasant'.

How can we be sure, though, that a patronizing attitude to writers like Scholz is justified? Is it reasonable to ignore such an accumulation of remarkable events, simply attributing them to chance? Could there not be hidden meaning in such conjunctions of events which makes them more than mere coincidences? Such questions were asked by a man who had sufficient stature to be taken seriously, namely Jung. He began to be greatly preoccupied with the problem presented by coincidences during the middle twenties, when he was elaborating his concept of the collective unconscious. Its contents, as will be recalled, were held to be primordial images of universal human themes, powerfully charged with psychic energy and emerging into consciousness in symbolic guise; these were the 'archetypes'. Whilst delving into these depths Jung encountered numerous connexions which, in his view, could not be adequately explained in terms of mere chance. One of these occurrences, which he cited more than once, will be quoted from the work in which he developed his ideas most fully:[13]

A young woman I was treating had, at a critical moment, a dream in which she was given a golden scarab. While she was telling me this dream I sat with my back to the closed window. Suddenly I heard a noise behind me like a gentle tapping. I turned round and saw a flying insect knocking against the window pane from outside. I opened the window and caught the creature in the air as it flew in. It was the nearest analogy to a golden scarab that one finds in our latitudes, a scarabaeid beetle, the common rose-chafer (Cetonia aurata), which contrary to its usual habits had evidently felt an urge to get into a dark room at this particular moment.

Personal experiences of this kind led him to the conviction that some special principle must be at work, which he set out to analyse and investigate. Jung named this principle 'synchronicity', defining it as a coincidence in time of two or more causally unrelated events which have the same or similar meaning. On the one hand, there is an inner experience, on the other an external event; these are linked meaningfully, though any causal connexion between them cannot even be imagined. It should be noted that the external events may take place not only at a distance, but also in the future, with only a present 'phantasm' corresponding to it. This enabled Jung to bring such phenomena as telepathy, clairvoyance and flying saucers within the scope of synchronicity. Since it would account for a much wider range of phenomena, including personal experiences, than the conventional scientific approach, synchronicity would bring us much closer to the beliefs about the universe held in traditional societies. Jung was of course aware of this, and if synchronicity is a valid principle, then much of what he called 'magical causality' would cease to be a chimera.

Mere assertion is of course not enough, and Jung, who saw his own role essentially as that of a scientist, knew very well that some kind of empirical demonstration of synchronicity in operation was necessary if he were to carry conviction. Hence he cast around for possible methods, considering first the *I Ching*; this is an ancient Chinese technique of divination, based on the patterns formed by the throwing of yarrow stalks, which later received a broader philosophical interpretation. It is closely similar to medieval Western geomancy, and to *Ifa* which is still practised in West Africa today. Jung eventually abandoned the idea of using the *I Ching*, because its outcome does not really lend itself to statistical treatment. Subsequently he decided to use astrology, and embarked on his so-called astrological experiment. The choice of this title was somewhat unfortunate, since it and some other ambiguous statements misled many of his readers into thinking that the purpose of the experiment was to test the validity of astrology; Jung later strenuously emphasized that it was in fact designed to provide an empirical basis for the notion of synchronicity.

In order to avoid the vagueness which the diagnosis of character would inevitably entail, Jung chose to concentrate on a hard fact, namely marriage. Certain conjunctions, such as those of sun and moon, are traditionally said by astrology to be associated with marriage; hence, if synchronicity operates, one would expect such conjunctions in the horoscopes of marriage partners significantly more often than among those of unmarried pairs. He proceeded to collect the horoscopes of 483 marriages, that is of nearly a thousand individuals, and subjected them to analysis. The expected conjunctions failed to turn up with a statistically significant frequency – in other words, one cannot be confident that the patterns were other than chance ones; nevertheless, there was some tendency in the direction Jung had expected, so that he felt justified in claiming synchronicity to have been at work. Now it is important to be quite clear what is involved: the numbers obtained from the horoscopes looked *as if* they were trying to make out the case for astrology; thus Jung was studying the behaviour of numbers under apparently chance conditions which offered scope for the play of synchronicity.

Having thus established the case, at least to his own satisfaction, Jung went on to discuss the logical status of the principle of synchronicity, placing it on a par with space, time and causality. Modern physics, he argued, has shown that natural laws are statistical in nature and only *relatively* true; thus there are spheres outside the realm of causality, and within these synchronicity holds sway. The occurrence of synchronistic phenomena is connected with the activation of the archetypes, so that we have a non-causal link between the psyche and the physical world.

So far I have merely attempted to outline Jung's ideas – admittedly in a grossly simplified manner, which robs his thought of its customary charm and subtlety; all the fascinating byways he explored with immense erudition have had to be omitted. I hope, nevertheless, that his central idea has been conveyed without undue distortion. Is it a revolutionary idea, unjustly neglected, or a sparkling intellectual bubble which so far hardly anybody has even bothered to try and puncture?

Perhaps an evaluation might start with the use to which the concept of synchronicity has been put by Jung and his followers. He said, 'Although meaningful coincidences are infinitely varied in their phenomenology, as acausal [i.e. not causally connected] events they nevertheless form an element that is part of the scientific picture of the world.' This scientific picture, it would probably be generally agreed, consists in the discovery of orderly relationships among phenomena, contributing to their understanding. By this criterion, what has been achieved through the use of the principle of synchronicity? In my own view, the answer would be 'very little, if anything'. It is true that synchronicity is often mentioned by Jung and the Jungians in discussing such things as extra-sensory perception, ghosts and apparitions as well as incidents in the course of psychotherapy similar to the one quoted. However, it does not seem to go beyond the function fulfilled by phlogiston in an earlier period – a mere verbal label serving as a pseudo-explanation. Let me try and substantiate this charge with reference to a book on apparitions and omens by Aniela Jaffé, mentioned in Chapter 2, that has the personal imprimatur of Jung. This consists of a large collection of reports of personal experiences of the paranormal. The author remains precariously balanced on the fence with regard to the objective truth or otherwise of these reports; ostensibly they are treated purely as psychological phenomena, but the language frequently betrays her conviction of the truth of at least some of them. What really matters, however, is the way in which these phenomena are interpreted in terms of synchronicity. We are told that they are manifestations of the archetypes, which produce a tendency to parallel events. It is the archetype which reveals itself as the sense or meaning in these events. The author goes on: 'In the "ordering" of synchronic events inner and outer, psychological and physical, subjective and objective, present and future facts are combined into a unity of experience and meaning.' There is a footnote warning the reader against the danger of lapsing into the old categories of causality, time and space, thereby being misled into thinking that the archetype *causes* the phenomena; it would be better to say, she assures us, that it *is* the phenomena.

Unless one is already among the converted, this will not do; one feels lost in an inextricable verbal morass, and the author must have some inkling of the readers' difficulties, for she likens the effort of grasping the notion of synchronicity to that required for the learning of a foreign language, which also demands the grasp of a foreign mentality. Indeed, those aspiring to a full apprehension of synchronicity are enjoined to return to a primitive magical mode of thinking merged with the unconscious, and at the same time to retain the capacity for critical thought. Whilst this is asking a lot, it is not as odd as it sounds; anthropological fieldwork demands something of this kind of capacity, albeit for a rather different purpose. The anthropologist attempts to penetrate a mode of thinking strange to him in order to establish its relationship to behaviour within a social system whose structure he wishes to assess. In contrast to this, what we are enjoined to do in order to understand synchronicity is to divide our own stream of thought, as it were, letting part of it flow into a dark swamp of phantasms, while the other part maintains an alert watch and yet accepts in some sense what Jaffé calls the 'magical realities'. Such a procedure is more likely to yield a specious sentiment of esoteric illumination than genuine insight.

If I am right in considering that, judging by the available instances, synchronicity fails as a helpful explanatory principle, this by itself does not dispose of the notion. It might still be true that Jung did discover a valid principle, but put it to uses for which it was not fitted. For in the first place meaningful co-incidences clearly occur – most of us have experienced them – and he also claimed to have provided proof of acausal synchronicity, through the astrological experiment. Hence it is desirable to return to this, looking at it more critically.

At the outset something further must be said about acausality, one of the key characteristics of synchronicity. Synchronistic events are inexplicable according to Jung not because we do not know the cause, but because a cause is not even thinkable in intellectual terms. Now with regard to astrology, Jung considered the possibility of 'a causal connexion between the planetary aspects of the psycho-physiological disposition', only to reject it; thus we are left with synchronicity. However, there is another alternative. Jung obtained the horoscopes from donors in Zurich, London, Rome and Vienna. These donors, it will be recalled, were married couples. Now Jung's argument assumes that there was no connexion between the planetary aspects at the birth of these people and their subsequent marriage. Yet since they were obviously interested in astrology, as indicated by the fact that they went to the trouble and expense of having their horoscopes cast, this assumption is questionable: in some cases at any rate the correspondence of the partners' horoscopes with the auspices traditionally regarded as favourable by astrology is likely to have entered as one element in the choice of marriage partner; if this applied to a minority, it could produce just the result obtained by Jung, namely a trend in the direction favouring astrology. Thus it is not necessary to have recourse to a far-fetched explanation based on the capricious behaviour of numbers conceived as in some way active agents.

In fact, there is evidence for the validity of this view. Jung's experiment was repeated by another investigator,[14] with a difference. Instead of collecting existing horoscopes of married couples, Arno Müller obtained his sample systematically from the records of the registrar's office in Freiburg. Astonishingly – one is tempted to make a trite remark about German thoroughness – in no less than 85 per cent of the marriages recorded the *hour* of birth of both partners was available. Müller then selected three years (1913, 1920, and 1925) and from among the marriages contracted during each of these years he secured data about the partners in 100 marriages that had endured until the date of the study, and another 100 that had ended in divorce. The main sample thus consisted of 600 married couples, supplemented by 326 cases where information was incomplete. He then computed the horoscopes of the 600 pairs, paying special attention to those factors which astrologers regard as relevant to the success of a union. The major focus of the study was a replication of Jung's 'astrological experiment', which involved the determination of the angular relationships of the constellations appertaining to each member of a married couple; unlike Jung, he found no tendency for those aspects traditionally regarded by astrologers as being important for marriage to be particularly marked.*

Apart from this, Müller analysed a series of factors alleged by astrologers to be favourable or otherwise to marriage prospects, and compared the enduring with the broken marriages on these factors. Only two out of a large number of comparisons emerged as statistically significant, and even these may be chance effects due to the extensive series of tests carried out. For instance, one factor emphasized by astrology is the mutual angular relationship between the positions of the sun at the births of the partners; the differences between enduring marriages and those that ended in divorce were well within the limit of chance fluctuations. Hence Müller arrived at the conclusions that 'the statistical

* Müller explicitly stated that, since his method of securing the sample presumably excluded the possible operation of synchronicity, his findings had no bearing on the Jungian hypothesis. I do not think that any conceivable procedure could exclude synchronicity in Jung's sense – it might have influenced the composition of the sample, for instance. Therefore I feel justified in using Müller's data as evidence against Jung.

evaluation did not confirm traditional astrological assumptions referring to marriage'.

Before leaving this topic it may be worth pointing out in passing that Jung must have moved in a circle intensely concerned with astrology, hence perhaps his statement that 'in no previous age . . . was astrology so widespread and generally accepted as in the present'; and he refers to a dinner party where he and his colleague were acquainted with the horoscopes of the guests.

Having dealt with the astrological experiment, we may now re-examine the scarab incident with a more sceptical eye. The story is presented in such a manner as to maximize its appearance of improbability, but it *can* be viewed somewhat differently. The patient, it will be recalled, had a dream in which she was given a golden scarab, and while she was telling this dream to Jung a similar insect flew against the window pane. Now perhaps it is not unfair to presume that it was the season of the year when rose-chafers were about; this fact might well have been causally connected with the patient's dream, the golden scarab being an elaboration of the actual sight of a rose-chafer; since many of them were about, it is perhaps not really very surprising that one of them bumped against the window, even though it was darker inside the room.

It may be objected that this exercise in causal analysis (or misguided effort to explain things away, as some may regard it) stops short at one crucial point: why did the rose-chafer knock just at that particular moment? The sceptic faced with this question may fall back somewhat lamely on chance, not without an uneasy feeling that there is possibly something to be explained here, and the principle of synchronicity would fill the bill. However, I believe that this question is of the have-you-stopped-beating-your-wife variety, which prejudges the issue; in order to show this it will be useful to reconsider Jung's view of the logical status of synchronicity.

The conventional dichotomy is between phenomena which are causal in nature and others where, after suitable statistical tests, one finds no reason to abandon the hypothesis that they are at random, i.e. due to chance. Jung further subdivided the latter into meaningless chance groupings as against meaningful coincidences; what he failed to provide is a clear guide as to the way in which these might be differentiated. He gives the instance of a tram ticket with the same number as a theatre ticket bought immediately afterwards, followed by an encounter with an identical phone number – this he would regard as a mere chance run. A series of six incidents involving fish (in conversations, inscriptions, embroidery, dreams), rounded off at the time of his writing by the finding of a dead fish, aroused in Jung the suspicion of meaningful coincidence. In explaining his eventual relegation of the fish series to the category of meaningless chance groupings he enunciated the rule that 'Runs ... which are composed of quite ordinary occurrences must for the present be regarded as fortuitous'. It would seem, therefore, that only 'extraordinary' occurrences qualify for the category of meaningful coincidence, but 'extraordinary' in what sense? There are at least two entirely distinct interpretations of this term: it may *either* be in the sense of an extremely low probability of the events concerned, *or* their unusual character and importance for the people involved. On the basis of the examples related by Jung it would seem to be the second; in the case already quoted the behaviour of the rose-chafer can hardly be regarded as highly improbable, the impression it created being due to the fact that it happened at an appropriate stage in the patient's treatment; similarly, in another example it was a flock of birds settling on a house, by itself not very extraordinary, whose effect was due to its association with a death. It may be suggested, therefore, that a coincidence is meaningful when it is experienced as such by the people affected; moreover, one can go a step further by saying that the meaning is imposed upon the pattern of events by the people involved.

Since there is a superficial resemblance between Jung's own and the alternative interpretation being put forward here – namely both being based on psychological processes – it will be useful to try to bring out the main distinction. Jung said that 'a content perceived by an observer can, at the same time, be represented by an outside event, without any causal connexion'. In terms of the illustration the patient's dream would be the content, and the simultaneous appearance of the rose-chafer the outside event.

When the situation is presented in this way, the question arises as to how this correspondence came about in the absence of any direct causal link; and Jung's answer is that the activation of the archetype in an emotionally charged situation synchronistically brought about the outside event.

The alternative interpretation proposed here rests upon a fundamental characteristic of human thinking, and indeed of human cognitive processes in general. This is the tendency to organize the environment into coherent patterns, to find meaning in the most diverse grouping of phenomena, and to derive satisfaction from such an achievement; conversely, an environment or events which fail to make sense are felt to be threatening and disturbing. The evidence for this is extensive, and only a few examples drawn from different spheres of behaviour will be briefly indicated. At the most elementary level, if people are presented with a random series of two symbols, it has been shown that in their responses they will tend to impose a structure where none really exists.[15] A film shows the following short sequence: a circle of light A approaches another stationary one B, stopping as soon as it comes into contact with the latter; B thereupon moves away in the same direction; asked to report what they saw, people answer 'A was pushing B'.[16] Devices for assessing the personality, such as the ink-blot test, a random shape into which people read their own meaning, are another instance. In a recent experiment two films were presented to an audience. One was concerned with a gruesome eye operation, the other a deliberately contrived set of nonsense sequence including such items as an aerial view of a toy battleship, a flushing toilet and a chess game played with cosmetic bottles. Although this was not the object of the exercise, it is relevant in the present context that viewers found both of these films equally anxiety-arousing and disturbing, as compared with an ordinary travel film.[17] In a stressful real-life setting, the reactions of patients and their families to the sudden onset of serious illness were studied. It was observed that there was a strong tendency for beliefs, often irrational, about the origin of the illness to develop. As a result of their study the investigators concluded that such beliefs serve an important purpose: 'A sense of mastery essential for functioning requires the discovery of meaning in an otherwise disordered and chaotic situation.'[18] It would be easy to multiply the list, as so many psychological studies directly or indirectly provide evidence of this principle, which has been summed up in a famous dictum by Sir Frederic Bartlett: '. . . it is fitting to speak of every human cognitive reaction – perceiving, imagining, remembering, thinking and reasoning – as an *effort after meaning*.'[19]

This universal human disposition has wider implications; but returning for a moment to Jung and synchronicity, I would suggest that one of its minor manifestations is the interest and mild elation we derive even from the more trivial coincidences, such as the identity of the numbers on a bus and a theatre ticket. We have discovered a pattern, and if the number happens to be that of our year of birth, its meaning is enhanced. It is not without significance that Jung used the expression 'chance groupings' as opposed to 'meaningful coincidences'; for the term 'meaningless coincidences' rings false, and is possibly a contradiction in terms. As long as there is no conscious awareness of chance groupings they might as well not exist, and many of us have probably missed the satisfaction of potential coincidences which escaped our attention. In fact, when discussing these problems with my colleagues, it was remarkable how each of us came across a heightened incidence of notable coincidences; the reason was not, I would submit, any sudden change in the nature of the physical world, but our increased sensitivity to patterns of similarity we would otherwise have ignored.

If this be accepted, the case of the scarab appears in an entirely different light. The fortuitous presence of the rose-chafer enabled Jung to capitalize on a chance event, relating this to the problem of his patient; it was certainly a curious coincidence which made this possible, but nothing miraculous; and Jung himself admitted the uniqueness of the experience. Let me hasten to add that I am far from wishing to impugn Jung's good faith – I have not the slightest doubt that he was utterly sincere, though in my opinion misguided, with regard to the concept of synchronicity. Being a highly gifted and creative psychiatrist, he possessed in an unusual manner the capacity for ordering phenomena in a rich variety of subtle ways, as is amply witnessed by his writings.

Jung was also intensely attuned to the thought of the ancients and of the Middle Ages, where elaborate edifices were commonly erected on the basis of resemblances and analogies, which today no longer form part of the structure of our formal reasoning; an example would be the idea of man as a microcosm, to which Jung was strongly attracted.

This idea of an intimate link between the macrocosm, the universe, and the microcosm, man, persisted until the scientific revolution of the seventeenth century. The notion of such a universal order or 'degree' still dominated the world of Elizabethan England. This could hardly be more succinctly epitomized than in the well-known speech by Ulysses in Shakespeare's *Troilus and Cressida*:

> The heavens themselves, the planets, and this centre,
> Observe degree, priority and place,
> Insisture, course, proportion, season, form,
> Office, and custom, all in line of order;
> And therefore is the glorious planet Sol
> In noble eminence enthron'd and spher'd
> Amidst the other, whose med'cinable eye
> Corrects the ill aspects of planets evil,
> And posts, like the commandment of a king,
> Sans check, to good and bad. But when the planets
> In evil mixture to disorder wander,
> What plagues and what portents, what mutiny,
> What raging of the sea, shaking of earth,
> Commotion in the winds! Frights, changes, horrors,
> Divert and crack, rend and deracinate,
> The unity and married calm of states
> Quite from this fixture! O, when degree is shak'd,
> Which is the ladder to all high designs,
> The enterprise is sick! How could communities,
> Degrees in schools, and brotherhoods in cities,
> Peaceful commerce from dividable shores,
> The primogenity and due of birth,
> Prerogative of age, crowns, sceptres, laurels,
> But by degree, stand in authentic place?

This 'magical view of nature', as I. A. Richards called it, not merely involved the idea of a general connexion between celestial and human affairs, but led to a detailed and fantastically elaborate working out of relationships.[20] The broad framework of this world view was fixed, but within it room could be made to accommodate new elements by assimilating them to the familiar; thus Red Indians were viewed as men from the traditional Golden Age, thereby weaving a fresh strand into the web, making it more colourful without breaking up the pattern. In such an intellectual climate which, in spite of its greater richness, is basically similar to that of pre-literate societies in their perspective on the cosmos, there is hardly room for the concept of coincidence. It is probably no accident that the first usage of the term in the sense of 'a notable concurrence of events or circumstances having no apparent causal connexion' is not recorded before the end of the seventeenth century. Tillyard vividly describes the importance of 'correspondences' for Elizabethans:

Not that the state of mind I am describing is extinct. In 1914, when Joffre and French were commanders-in-chief, many people were truly delighted that each name contained six letters and that the last three letters of the first name and the first three of the second were identical. But in Elizabethan times the coincidence would have been felt to be truly portentous. Indeed the amount of intellectual and emotional satisfaction these correspondences then afforded is difficult both to imagine and to overestimate. What to us is merely silly might for an Elizabethan be a solemn or joyful piece of evidence that he lived in an ordered universe where there was no waste and where every detail was part of nature's plan. (p. 105.)

The advent of the scientific revolution in the West gradually destroyed such harmonious and satisfying modes of thinking, widening the separation between self and the world which Piaget traced in childhood. Although the new patterns produced by scientific thought are not devoid of the qualities that made the old order so attractive, they gratify in the main only a minority. No wonder Jung felt that we had suffered a loss, in which he felt he could discern one of the main sources of our present malaise. He looked back nostalgically, and attempted to construct a bridge which would have brought the two worlds together; for the scientific minority it is too late, and the lost paradise cannot be regained. For them the touchstone is not the internal harmony

& & also the birth rate peak @ the time of the big New York black out.

among ideas, but the demonstrable relationship between ideas and the external world; and in this synchronicity is found wanting.

While scientific modes of thinking are properly distinguished from the older magical world view, it is important to remind ourselves that ultimately both share the conception of order and uniformity in nature, as was already recognized by Frazer; and this in turn is rooted in the fundamental characteristics of human thinking. When it comes to the frontiers of knowledge, this family resemblance is easier to discern. Advances sometimes take place by imaginative leaps, with the laborious collection of evidence lagging behind. Observations in little-known fields are sometimes difficult to interpret, and what one makes of them then largely depends on personal beliefs. This is most clearly apparent in a statistical concept that is in some ways analogous to coincidence, namely correlation, which is a measure of the extent to which two phenomena vary together in the same or the opposite direction. One might say that coincidence is a conjunction of two events, correlation one of two series of events. The crucial question often is whether or not a correlation reflects a genuine causal relationship, and in the absence of any other evidence it may not be easy to decide. This is because there can be nonsense correlations, due either to chance or a trivial underlying factor. For instance, over the period 1875 to 1920 there was an extremely high inverse correlation between the birth rate in Britain and the production of pig iron in the United States, the former falling to almost exactly the same extent as the latter rose. The simple explanation in this case is that both were regular trends over time.

N.B

Let us take a more interesting correlation, however, which recaptures the flavour of some ancient astrological ideas. In 1959 a letter was published in the distinguished scientific journal *Nature* reporting a correlation between the transit of Uranus across the meridian and the occurrence of severe earthquakes on our planet. Subsequently a mathematician criticized the method and questioned the inference in the absence of any firm theory to account for the alleged relationship. The original author concluded his reply as follows:

The earthquake which destroyed Agadir on February 29 of this year occurred with Uranus only about 4° from the meridian. Anybody in Agadir, knowing of my communication to *Nature*, and being warned by the preceding minor shocks and the reported behaviour of animals, would have kept away from buildings at the time of Uranus being near the meridian, which was from about 10 hr. to 12 hr., a.m. or p.m. The destruction of the town occurred at 11 hr. p.m. local time. An unbiased approach to these problems, of which the correlations of Uranus are only a part and a first step, may help humanity.[21]

Was it mere chance that the Agadir earthquake fitted in with the correlations previously observed, or does this indicate the existence of a physically identifiable causal connexion? The scientific mode of thinking involves the ability to suspend judgement until the evidence tips the balance. Ordinary thinking (and this of course also applies to scientists *qua* members of the community, outside their special field) is more liable to jump the gap and close the pattern. In our own society in the past, and traditional sections of some societies at present, gaps were not even allowed to occur and every phenomenon found its place in a meaningful whole. This served to reduce uncertainty and doubt, to whose relationship to superstition we shall now turn.

N.B.

REFERENCES

1 John Beattie, *Other Cultures*, London: Cohen & West, 1964, p. 7.
2 Sir E. B. Tylor, *The Origins of Culture*, London: Murray, 1871. Quoted from Harper Torchbook edn., New York, 1958, p. 134.
3 Lucien Lévy-Bruhl, *How Natives Think*, Allen, 1926.
4 E. E. Evans-Pritchard, *Witchcraft, Oracles and Magic among the Azande*, Oxford: Clarendon Press, 1937, p. 65.
5 A detailed exposition is given by John H. Flavell (*The Developmental Psychology of Jean Piaget*, London: Van Nostrand, 1963).
6 Jean Piaget, *The Child's Conception of the World*, Kegan Paul, 1929.
7 An extensive survey of such observations is presented in the work of Heinz Werner (*Comparative Psychology of Mental Development*, New York: International Universities Press, 1957). See Chapter 11, 'The Fundamental Ideas of Magic'.
8 Iona and Peter Opie, *The Lore and Language of Schoolchildren*, Oxford University Press, 1959, Chapter 11, 'Half-belief'.
9 See G. Jahoda, 'Child animism I and II', *Journal of Social Psychology*, 1958, 47, pp. 197–222.
10 'African traditional thought and western science', *Africa*, 1967, 37, pp. 50–71 and 155–87.

11 H. A. L. Hart and A. M. Honoré, *Causation in the Law*, Oxford University Press, 1959, p. 74.

12 Wilhelm von Scholz, *Der Zufall und das Schicksal*, München: Paul List, 1959.

13 C. G. Jung and W. Pauli, *The Interpretation of Nature and the Psyche*, Kegan Paul, 1955, p. 31.

14 Arno Müller, 'Eine statistische Untersuchung astrologischer Faktoren bei dauerhaften und geschiedenen Ehen', *Zeitschrift für Parapsychologie*, 1958, 1, pp. 93–101.

15 H. W. Hake and R. Hyman, 'Perception of the statistical structure of a random series of binary symbols', *Journal of Experimental Psychology*, 1953, 45, pp. 64–74.

16 A. Michotte, *La Perception de la Causalité*, Louvain: Publications Universitaires, 1954.

17 Don Byrne and G. L. Clore, 'Effectance arousal and attraction', *Journal of Personality and Social Psychology*, 1967, Monograph No. 638.

18 M. Bard and R. B. Dyk, 'The psychodynamic significance of beliefs regarding the cause of serious illness', *Psychoanalytic Review*, 1956, 43, pp. 146–63.

19 *Remembering*, Cambridge University Press, 1932, p. 44.

20 This has been admirably described by E. M. W. Tillyard (*The Elizabethan World Picture*, Penguin Books, 1963).

21 *Nature*, 23.4.60, pp. 337–8.

CHAPTER EIGHT

Superstition and Uncertainty

Men would never be superstitious, if they could govern all their circumstances by set rules, or if they were always favoured by fortune: but being frequently driven into straits where rules are useless, and being often kept fluctuating pitiably between hope and fear by the uncertainty of fortune's greedily coveted favours, they are consequently, for the most part, very prone to credulity.

Spinoza *Tractatus Theologico-Politicus*

These words of Spinoza anticipate in essence by some two-and-a-half centuries a theory of magic propounded by the famous anthropologist Bronislaw Malinowski. He started from the observation that the world of primitive man may be broadly divided into two spheres. Given a certain stock of knowledge and skills, one of these can be mastered and controlled in such a way that man can satisfy his needs; outside this sphere, the competence available is insufficient by itself to ensure the attainment of man's goals, and it is here that magic holds sway. Malinowski's frequently cited example relates to the fishing practices of the inhabitants of the Trobriand Archipelago, where he undertook his major fieldwork. Those in villages on the inner lagoon, where fishing is easy and safe, do not have any magical procedures associated with it; by contrast villages on the open sea could obtain fish only in circumstances that were hazardous and highly uncertain. This illustrates Malinowski's main point that 'man resorts to magic only where chance and circumstances are not fully controlled by knowledge'.

While Malinowski's theory cannot be examined here in detail, it should be mentioned that critics[1] have rightly raised some important objections to the all-embracing nature of his claims. In the first place, the division of the world into the two spheres of controllable and capricious is by no means easy. Thus one might have thought that for the Trobrianders, living on a tropical island, the growing of crops would be relatively straightforward and fall into the former category, not needing any magic; yet in fact, magic was extensively used in the cultivation of their gardens. It can be shown that there is a whole range of magical and related supernatural beliefs and practices, including several described by Malinowski himself, that do not fit readily into his theoretical scheme. Maleficent magic, witchcraft and other aspects concerned with social relationships (see Chapter 6 above) are particularly important examples. This does not necessarily mean that Malinowski's theory is totally false, but it does seem to stand in need of a more circumspect formulation. Perhaps I might suggest the following: where chance and circumstances are not fully controlled by knowledge, man is more likely to resort to magic. When the theory is rephrased in this way, it loses its apparent precision, but tends to fall into line with widely held popular notions. These are that certain types of occupations involving risk, uncertainty or fear are particularly liable to superstition. Among these are sailors, soldiers and the theatrical profession. As far as I know, there have been no systematic studies of the differential incidence of superstitions for people in different occupations, but the prevalence among soldiers in war has been documented in the monumental study on *The American Soldier* during the Second World War.[2] Numerous superstitious practices of combat men have been reported there. These include wearing protective charms and amulets, like a medal or a rabbit's foot. Certain supposedly unlucky actions such as 'three on a match' were carefully avoided. Many soldiers used a variety of protective superstitions simultaneously and explained them by saying that though it might be silly there was no harm in it and anyway, there might be something in it. Two practices are of special interest: 'They might carry out pre-battle preparations in a fixed, "ritual" order. They might jealously keep articles of clothing or equipment which were associated with some past experience of escape from danger.'

This is the kind of behaviour that might be predicted on the basis of Skinner's theory: the particular series of actions or the possession of particular items of equipment happened to be powerfully reinforced and are therefore rigidly maintained prior to subsequent exposure to threatening situations.

It is reported also that in certain historical situations, and notably the plague epidemics, there was a vast upsurge of superstitions. In his fictional but horrifyingly accurate *Journal of the Plague Year* Daniel Defoe described this vividly:

These terrors and apprehensions of the people led them into a thousand weak, foolish and wicked things, which there wanted not a sort of people, really wicked, to encourage them to; and this was running about to fortune-tellers, cunning men and astrologers, to know their fortune, or, as it is vulgarly expressed, to have their fortunes told them, their nativities calculated, and the like, and this folly presently made the town swarm with a wicked generation of Pretenders to Magic, to the *Black Art*, as they called it, and I know not what; nay, to a thousand worse dealings with the Devil than they were really guilty of; and this trade grew so open, and was so generally practised, that it became common to have signs and inscriptions set up at doors: 'Here lives a Fortune-teller', – 'Here lives an Astrologer', – 'Here you may have your nativity calculated', – and the like; and Friar *Bacon*'s Brazen Head, which was the usual sign of these people's dwellings, was to be seen in almost every street, or else the sign of Mother *Shipton*, or of *Merlin*'s head, and the like.

While this is only an imaginative account, Defoe had his facts right, as is confirmed by many contemporary records relating to outbreaks of the plague in various parts of Europe.

It is not really useful to multiply the anecdotal evidence, which strongly suggests an increase in superstition when the environment becomes more uncontrollable. There is at least one systematic study of the same problem, dealing with dowsing.[3] This is a practice of considerable antiquity, designed to locate underground water (or minerals) by means of a cleft twig which dips over the right spot. Apparently this method, regarded by a majority of competent scientists as superstitious, remains widely prevalent in the country which is in the van of scientific and technological advance, the twentieth-century United States. Hence the authors, psychologist and anthropologist respectively, felt that this was a particularly suitable topic for investigating the roots of superstitious behaviour. They took as their starting-point the theory of Malinowski expounded above, and on this basis evolved the following hypothesis:

We would expect to find that witching [American usage for 'dowsing'] is common wherever the outcome of well-digging is highly uncertain; on the other hand, we would not expect water witching to be practised where ground-water conditions and geological knowledge make the outcome highly predictable.

In order to test this hypothesis, they selected a representative sample of US counties and classified them according to ground-water regions as defined by the US geological survey, arranging them into an order of difficulty of locating water. They then obtained information from the agricultural extension agents in the counties about the number of 'witches' practising in the area. On the average they found some 18 witches per 100,000 population which, extrapolated, means that there seems to be a sizeable total of about 25,000 in the United States. In general, they discovered a close relationship between the difficulty with which ground-water can be located, and the percentage of diviners in the population. Apart from this, they also uncovered a lot of fascinating information about the procedures employed, and the characteristics of the water witches. The main thing is of course that the hypothesis was confirmed, and the results, in the words of the authors, '. . . are consistent with the theory that magic serves an important function, and with the view that witching is a ritual that reduces anxiety in the same way that magic does in non-literate societies'.

Elsewhere the writers were less cautious and seem to imply that they had tested and confirmed Malinowski's original theory, which is not the case; in order to do so, one would have to show that all forms of magic conform to this pattern, and there is ample evidence against this. The authors also raise the interesting questions whether dowsing as a type of magic is *ipso facto* a form of irrational behaviour. Now of course the answer depends at least in part on the way one chooses to define rational behaviour, on which there is little agreement. A great deal of present-day research on decision-making requires some sort of rational behaviour, and the gordic knot is usually cut by assuming that the rational individual will make the choice that maximizes his expected utility or, in the more homely translation of this phrase by Hyman and Vogt 'gives him the best run for his money'. Given such a conception of rationality, it is easy to envisage circumstances in which the choice of dowsing could be rational: where no adequate scientific information is available; and where there is some reason, however slender, for believing that a dowser might improve the chances of locating a well. The second condition may quite often apply. If a dowser has worked in an area for some time he is likely, irrespective of any supposed supernatural gift, to acquire some knowledge of the kind of local terrain where drilling will tend to be successful or otherwise. In this he would have an advantage over an outside geologist who could only draw broad inferences from the gross structure of the region, and would hardly be able to commit himself to indicate the precise point at which to sink a well.

We have thus reached the somewhat surprising conclusion that magic may sometimes work in practice; and this relates not to the psychological effects previously discussed, but to effectiveness in the technological sense. Much the same argument has been put forward by Moore[4] in connexion with certain modes of divination. He suggested that 'some practices which have been classified as magic may well be directly efficacious as techniques for attaining the ends envisaged by their practitioners'. The example analysed by Moore is based on a description of divination among Indians in Labrador. They are hunters, and failure to track down the game is catastrophic for them and results in hunger and possibly death. When food is short through lack of success, these Indians consult an oracle to determine the directions the hunt should take. For this purpose, the shoulder blade of a caribou is held over hot coals, and the cracks and spots caused by the heat are then interpreted like a map. The directions indicated by this oracle tend to be approximately random. Now why should this be regarded as an efficacious method?

131

The ingenious argument developed by Moore runs roughly as follows: if they did not use the oracle, the decisions of the Indians about where to hunt would probably be largely influenced by success in the past. This would lead to areas that have been over-hunted, and are thus devoid of game. Moreover, any regularity in the behaviour of the hunters gives the animals a chance of learning where danger threatens, and taking appropriate avoiding action. By randomizing their forays through the oracle, the regular pattern is broken up and the chances of reaching game are increased. Although plausible, this theory is admittedly somewhat speculative. In support of his thesis Moore points out that these Indians are highly dependent on killing game, and from an evolutionary perspective it is unlikely that a poor and ineffective method would have had survival value, and itself survived.

This is of course a rather special case, and the approach was used by the Indians only when they had no firm information as to where game was located; whenever they did have such information, they acted upon it. In one important sense, uncertainty is equivalent to shortage or absence of information on which a decision may be based. This notion is linked to that of control over the environment, since the more information we have at our disposal, the more likely we are to be able to deal effectively with our environment. Hence information has a positive value, and there is some evidence that this may even be true at the animal level. Prokasy[5] used a maze with a single choice point, from which two paths led to goal boxes; these were out of sight even after the rat had chosen the right or left path. The chances of food being in either of the boxes were even. But on one side the rat was provided with information whether there would be food in the goal box or not; this was done by painting the passage black or white as a consistent signal. After some days of training the rats developed a preference for that part of the maze where they obtained advance information, even though the frequency and amount of food obtained there were no greater than in the other half.

Much the same preference for information about the outcome, whether this be reward or punishment, has been demonstrated in human subjects.[6] Again the preference was shown in spite of the fact that people derived no advantage from it other than learning what was going to happen in any case. These findings are of course in line with everyday life experience. During general elections, many people sit up a large part of the night to see results coming in, and listen to the forecasts of psephologists; all this serves no purpose at all other than reducing their uncertainty as soon as possible, since they could otherwise hear the outcome in the morning without losing any sleep. This desire to know what is in store helps to account for the widespread resort to prophecy and divination in practically all known societies; as is evident from the material on prevalence in Chapter 2, showing how many people patronize fortune-tellers or at least scan the astrological columns in the numerous newspapers and magazines that carry them, the same need continues to be catered for in much the same way in advanced industrial countries. The anxiety to know one's fate is so great that often ill tidings may be preferred to an absence of information, and after a period of anxious waiting even bad news may come as something of a relief, because it frees a person to adjust actively to a situation. Thus prisoners who had a chance of release were found in an American study to be under greater strain than those who had none, and were reconciled to the fact. In circumstances where numbers of people are together without adequate information, such as concentration or prisoner-of-war camps, a series of rumours almost invariably arises. Although most of these tend to be largely untrue, they do at least serve to still for a while the suffering caused by uncertainty. Observations of people in such conditions as well as the experimental results indicate that there are considerable individual differences in tolerance of uncertainty; some endure it stoically even in matters of life and death, while others find it almost unbearable with regard to relatively trivial issues, such as whether or not they are going to get an invitation to a party.

At the same time it would be rash to conclude that men strive after a state of complete certainty, with full information and control. Man as a biological organism is equipped to cope with variability in his environment. The kind of state envisaged by

Spinoza whereby rigid following of set rules would automatically ensure success would be an intolerable burden which man could not endure. Many converging lines of evidence[7] indicate this, and perhaps one example from the sphere of aesthetics may be cited. If subjects are presented with random shapes differing in complexity of structure,[8] they characteristically dislike both the very simple and straightforward as well as the extremely complex ones, settling for an intermediary amount of cognitive uncertainty. It was shown that people are sensitive to differences in variability of stimuli, getting rapidly bored with those that are readily predictable. This again is in accord with common wisdom, for we know that many forms of uncertainty and risk, such as gambling or mountaineering, have a positive attraction for men, so that they actually seek them out. Reduction of uncertainty is thus not an end in itself, and beyond a certain level may in fact become highly undesirable: after all, few conditions in human life are more predictable than the prison routine, yet it is distinctly lacking in attraction!

Some experimental studies have also demonstrated variations in the emotional concomitants of uncertainty. New and highly threatening situations are apt to arouse anxiety, and the less known about the probable outcome, the more intense the anxiety. In such circumstances there tends to be a strong desire for both information and some means of control. In the words of Pervin,[9] who carried out one of the most valuable studies in this field:

> While some authors have emphasized the usefulness of activity *per se* in controlling anxiety, the results here would suggest that the psychological meaning of the activity is significant. It may be suggested that activity involving the feeling of participation in the turn of events, with the hope of mastery, is preferable to and less anxiety-arousing than no activity at all or activity which leaves the person feeling a helpless victim of inevitable events.

One is forcibly struck by the fact of how well superstition fits the bill here, since it provides at least the subjective feeling of predictability and control. It may thus serve the function of reducing anxiety: and as intense anxiety is liable to inhibit effective action in dangerous situations, there is a distinct possi-

N B

bility that superstition may have positive survival value in certain circumstances. If this reasoning is valid, it contributes to our understanding why certain classes of people (miners, sailors, air pilots, actors) exposed to great risks of physical or professional disaster tend to be more superstitious than others not exposed to such hazards. Although we do not yet know enough about this whole problem, it looks as though one has to think in terms of complex sets of interactions between levels of uncertainty and risk in the situation, and the characteristics of the individual concerned. The man who goes in for a mild flutter has no need for superstition; but the inveterate gambler for high stakes, painted so vividly by Dostoyevsky in his (largely autobiographical) novel *The Gambler*, is notoriously superstitious. Perhaps this is not a particularly good example, since Dostoyevsky's own superstition (or 'secret' as he called it) was that if one does not get excited in the course of a game, one is bound to win. This magical formula which included anxiety as one of its terms was of course self-defeating, but his constant and substantial losses in no way shook his faith; if only he could maintain perfect composure, he would without any doubt have 'overcome the stupidity of blind chance and won his game'.

One notion which often crops up in relation to gambling is that of 'luck'. It has been lucidly analysed by John Cohen,[10] and there would be little purpose in going over the ground he has covered. There are, however, a few additional observations to be made, some of them based on recent investigations on behaviour in situations of uncertainty. In one of these people were presented with hypothetical problems of the following kind:

A hungry rat is placed in a maze with two arms. The experimenter places a piece of meat sometimes in the left and sometimes in the right arm of the maze; it also happens that occasionally he puts meat on both sides or on neither. On each trial the meat is placed in a random sequence, and the placings on each occasion are quite independent; but on the average there is one piece out of three on the left-hand side, and two out of three on the right. What ought to be the behaviour of the rat so that it should have as much food as possible, given that it can only go either right or left on each trial?[11]

Now the rational strategy in this type of case, which will maximize the outcome for the chooser, is to go consistently for the alternative which has a 2/3 probability. It emerged that people who were able to recognize the rational strategy were much less likely to hold a belief in luck. This is not an unexpected finding, implying as it does that where people are deficient in the rational understanding of an uncertain environment they have a greater tendency to resort to superstitious ideas.

Yet there are psychologists who take an entirely different view of the matter, and appear willing to take 'luck' seriously.[12] One of them in particular is a well-known Dutch psychologist, Director of the Netherlands Foundation for Industrial Psychology and thence, one presumes, fairly hard-headed. In an article on success or failure in industry he wrote:

> There are clear indications that some people have a certain flair for attracting good fortune, in addition to all the factors mentioned previously. They seem to have been born 'under a lucky star', if this archaic expression is permissible, whereas others seem to have a continuous run of bad luck. Some people seem to attract good fortune, others never rise to the occasion and cannot but fail ... Perhaps we are confronted here with the deepest and most fundamental relation between man and his environment.[13]

My own reaction to this was at the time simply to dismiss it with the thought: here we have a superstitious psychologist! Subsequently I came across a laboratory experiment that made me pause. This was presented to the participants as an experiment in extra-sensory perception. Subjects were asked to guess the sequence of colours in a shuffled pack of playing cards. After a preliminary run, those scoring high (lucky) were separated from those scoring low (unlucky). So far there is nothing unexpected or out of the ordinary about this. The next stage, however, was for the groups to engage in another round of guessing of colours. Now by chance one would expect both groups to do equally well on repetition of the task; in fact the 'lucky' group continued to do significantly better than the unlucky group! As the author[14] cautiously put it 'this data provides some empirical support for the popular notion of luck'. Perhaps it may after all be rash to dismiss the possibility of 'luck' attaching to particular individuals out of hand. This does not mean that I am now convinced,

136 ✗ what about games
psychology .. losers & winners etc.

because in a case like this the evidence one requires is particularly stringent – there may have been unknown snags in the procedure that vitiated the outcome.[15]

Nonetheless, we have now come full circle, and end by repeating the initial warning that superstition is a relative concept, dependent on the state of scientific knowledge at a particular point of time. It may be that in future child-training manuals will contain instructions helping parents to ensure that their offspring will be endowed with the quality of 'luck'.

REFERENCES

1 For instance E. R. Leach and S. F. Nadel in R. Firth (ed.), *Man and Culture*, Routledge, 1957.
2 Samuel A. Stouffer *et al.*, *The American Soldier: combat and its aftermath*, vol. II, Princeton University Press, 1949, pp. 188ff.
3 Ray Hyman and Evon Z. Vogt, 'Water Witching: Magical Ritual in Contemporary United States', *Psychology Today*, 1967, 1, pp. 35-42.
4 Omar Khayyam Moore, 'Divination – a new perspective', *American Anthropologist*, 1957, 59, pp. 69-74.
5 W. F. Prokasy, 'The acquisition of observing responses in the absence of differential external reinforcement', *Journal of Comparative Physiological Psychology*, 1956, 49, pp. 131-4.
6 See for instance John T. Lanzetta and James M. Driscoll, 'Preference for information about an uncertain but unavoidable outcome', *Journal of Personality and Social Psychology*, 1966, 3, pp. 96-102.
7 D. O. Hebb, *The Organization of Behavior*, New York: Wiley, 1949; S. Maddi, 'Affective tone during environmental regularity and change', *Journal of Abnormal and Social Psychology*, 1961, 62, pp. 338-45.
8 Harry Munsingh and William Kessen, 'Uncertainty structure, and preference', *Psychological Monographs*, 1964, No. 586, 78, No. 9.
9 Lawrence A. Pervin, 'The need to predict and control under conditions of threat', *Journal of Personality*, 1963, 31, pp. 570-87.
10 John Cohen, *Chance, Skill and Luck*, Penguin Books, 1960.
11 R. Lambert and M. Zaleska, 'Choix d'une stratégie en fonction du mode de présentation d'une série aléatoire imaginaire de fréquence connue et déterminants du comportement rationnel', *Bulletin du C.E.R.P.*, 1966, 15, pp. 17-38.
12 J. Ohana, *La Chance*, Paris: Presses Universitaires de France, 1948.
13 D. J. van Lennep, 'Why some succeed and others fail', *Progress*, 1962, 48, pp. 270-74.
14 Richard L. Taylor, 'Habitual short-term expectancies and luck', *Journal of General Psychology*, 1967, 76, pp. 81-4.
15 'Very few scientists would accept a theory based on superstition, even if it received a factor of 1000 from the first experiment' [i.e. had a very high apparent probability of being an outcome due to factors other than chance]. I. J. Good, in *Probability and the Weighing of Evidence*, London: Griffin, 1950, p. 83.

CHAPTER NINE

The Future of Superstition

Prodigies, omens, oracles, judgements quite obscure the few natural events that are intermingled with them. But as the former grow thinner every page, in proportion as we advance nearer the enlightened ages, we soon learn, that there is nothing mysterious or supernatural in the case, but that all proceeds from the usual propensity of mankind towards the marvellous; and that though this inclination may at intervals receive a check from sense and learning, it can never be thoroughly extirpated from human nature.

David Hume *Essays*

In isolated pre-literate cultures, where superstitious beliefs form an integral part of people's total outlook on the world, nearly everybody believes nearly everything. This, as has been shown, is because alternatives are not readily conceivable by individuals. However, such a state of affairs is becoming increasingly rare today, with few communities remaining untouched by external influences. Over most of the globe now it is more characteristic to find a mixture: some people take socially transmitted superstitions seriously, while others laugh at them; some claim to have occult experiences, others are sceptics. My guess would be that everybody has his own personal 'Skinnerian' superstitions, whether they are prepared to admit them or not. The most striking factors, though, are the variations in the incidence of superstitious beliefs and behaviour. Some of the theories discussed help to throw some light on this problem. Thus on the Freudian interpretation one would expect certain kinds of neurotics to be more superstitious than normals. There is a certain amount of support for this from studies carried out during the

1930s, when 'superstitiousness' was frequently regarded as a personality trait. Allport[1] in his famous work listed it among his 'common traits', together with such others as emotional maturity, honesty and originality. Several measures of this trait were mentioned in a handbook edited by J. McV. Hunt,[2] and a significant relationship was reported between one of these and tests of neurotic tendencies. Yet on the whole what these measures accomplish is merely to assess the extent, if any, to which superstition is present, without helping to explain either its origin within the individual, or the differences between individuals.

The only study known to me that seeks to probe this question, albeit as a by-product rather than a major objective, is the monumental investigation of the authoritarian personality.[3] The impetus for this study came from the virulent persecutions of Nazi rule, which led to a concerted attempt on the part of this distinguished group of social scientists to discover the roots of prejudice from which such behaviour sprang. The work is widely known, and only enough need be said about it to provide an adequate context. They devised scales for assessing prejudice, administered these to a wide range of people, and then subjected groups at either extreme (i.e. highly prejudiced and highly tolerant) to an intensive clinical study. Their scales included items of the following type:

Although many people may scoff, it may yet be shown that astrology can explain a lot of things.

It is more than a remarkable coincidence that Japan had an earthquake on Pearl Harbor Day, 7 December, 1944.

It was found that the highly prejudiced were also more prone to superstition, and this fits in with the type of home background which, according to the clinical interviews, was characteristic of them. It was one with a relatively harsh and threatening discipline, where parents exercised a rigid control which was not permitted to be questioned, although it was experienced as arbitrary. This seems consistent with the development of a belief that one's fate is in the hands of unknown external powers, governed by forces over which one has no control. Naturally one has to guard against drawing excessively sweeping conclusions from such findings, but it does look as though a tyrannical and arbitrary home background is likely to produce a predisposition towards the acceptance of superstition. A complicating element here is the fact that a majority of the highly prejudiced were relatively low in social class, educational level and intelligence, which may all have contributed. Some indication of this comes from a recent test[4] designed to assess the extent to which individuals feel themselves to be masters of their own destiny or puppets on an invisible string; people low in social class tended more towards the latter category. Does this mean that they are more superstitious? We can look at some evidence, from the work of Gorer quoted in Chapter 2, where percentage of belief in various kinds of superstition has been broken down by income-group, and some of this is reproduced in the table below. In every case the belief is most commonly held by the lowest income-group, declining somewhat irregularly but on the whole consistently as one moves to the right. So it seems that there may be something in the connexions discussed, but so far it is little more than speculation, nor can we be sure of the causal relations involved.

The prevalence of working-class superstition is graphically portrayed in Richard Hoggart's book *The Uses of Literacy*. While this does not pretend to be a rigorous inquiry, it is a social document based largely on first-hand experience and as such

Per cent Belief in Particular Superstitions by Income Groups

(After Geoffrey Gorer, *Exploring English Character*, Cresset Press, 1955.)

	Income				
	Low end			High end	
Believe in ghosts	23	17	15	16	16
Heard or seen ghost (among believers only)	63	40	34	45	30
Has lucky mascot	18	16	14	14	16
Has lucky day	13	9	7	9	6
Has lucky number	26	17	17	16	19
Been to fortune-teller	53	44	41	41	40
Reads horoscopes regularly	51	45	42	41	29
Think there is something in it	24	19	13	16	16

commands attention. Hoggart describes how a large variety of relatively minor superstitions, about good luck and bad luck, dreams and health, pervade everyday life. In his own words, 'The world of experience is mapped at every point', and Hoggart concludes by explaining that while working-class people often laugh at the superstitions and disclaim beliefs they do by and large abide by the route shown on the map: 'They go on repeating the old tags and practising their sanctions and permissions.'

It is tempting to infer that superstition is a mere survival in our kind of society. Working-class people, being less educated, cling to them longer, but sooner or later they will die out altogether. This is a rather common notion among people who regard themselves as enlightened. The author of the one book known to me with precisely the same title as the present one[5] ends it on the same comforting note. Certain types of behaviour which could at one time have been considered as superstition lost their supernatural significance and now remain nothing more than empty gestures. An example would be blessing someone who has sneezed. Originally it was felt necessary to do this, since the soul was thought to have left the body temporarily, and the blessing helped to make sure that it returned to its proper abode. Today the content, namely the superstitious experience that once accompanied the act, is dead. And so to his final peroration: 'Such is the path – a very indirect one – whereby the constant evolution towards rational experience eventually succeeds in vanquishing some part of superstition and, in the future, will progressively deprive it of life . . .

There are others who feel more strongly on this issue, seeing in superstition an example of the shortcomings of human mental processes which must be overcome. For instance Chisholme[6] in a symposium on future developments regarding man used superstitions, as taught in childhood and carried into maturity, as examples of what he called 'the kind of misuse of the function of the mind which produces most of man's major problems and now threatens his existence'. Or again, a notable historian of science declared that the history of superstition, as opposed to that of science which is instructive and encouraging, 'can prove nothing except the imbecility of the human mind'. On this view, which is not uncommon, superstition is nothing but a manifestation of human gullibility and folly, a monster which we must slay to ensure progress or even survival; and the weapon most frequently advocated to combat and ultimately defeat it is education.[7]

Opinions of this kind are themselves irrational in nature. They are not the outcome of a dispassionate analysis of the phenomenon, but little more than an unreflective response to the pejorative flavour of the label. Superstition is thereby identified with error, or lack of information. The shortcomings of such a view and the fallacy of castigating the ideas and beliefs of another era as superstitious have already been discussed. After all, the forerunners of the scientific revolution, from Roger Bacon to Kepler, until well into the seventeenth century, retained magical and esoteric beliefs while heralding a new approach to the physical universe. Surely it would be absurd to reproach them with imbecility merely because in some respects they were children of their time! A striking example of the coexistence of two apparently quite disparate modes of thinking within the same skull was the brilliant German mathematician Michael Stifler, who improved the algebraic symbolism, was one of the inventors of Pascal's triangle, and adumbrated the notion of logarithms. This man was converted by Luther and became a fanatical adherent, predicting the end of the world. He claimed that Pope Leo X was the Beast of the Apocalypse, and proved it to his own and many of his eminent contemporaries' satisfaction by means of 'gematria', a form of numerology facilitated by the fact that letters in several alphabets, including of course the Roman, have numerical values. Here is how the demonstration went, keeping in mind that the number of the Beast is 666 (Revelation 13, xviii):

$$\begin{array}{cccccc} \text{Leo} & \text{De} & \text{C} & \text{I} & \text{M} & \text{Vs} \\ 50 + & 500 + & 100 + & 1 + & 1000 + & 5 = 1656 \end{array}$$

Take away M(ysterium) -1000
Add (Leo) X $+10$
          $\overline{666}$

Therefore Leo X = The Beast

Looking at this through modern eyes one is inclined to marvel how this kind of puerility could be reconciled with mathematical genius; indeed, one commentator suggested that his mind might have become deranged by excessive bigotry, though adding that many other men of the period seem to have been equally crazy. It is possible, however, to take an entirely different standpoint, implicit in a now somewhat outmoded debate concerning the relationships of magic, religion and science. Some writers used to maintain that magic was the source from which both religion and science sprang simultaneously, others supporting a sequence from magic via religion to science. All such schemes involve a recognition of common elements between magic and science, in the sense of postulating some scheme of order and regularity in the world. From the psychological angle, the underlying thought processes are unlikely to be basically different: both lead to the establishment of relationships on the basis of perception of likeness, recognition of resemblances in superficially distinct phenomena, and analogical reasoning. D'Arcy Thompson expressed this pithily: 'Newton did not show the cause of the apple falling but he showed a similitude between the apple and the stars.' Darwin's close study of artificial selection by breeders led him to a search for analogous processes in nature which would account for variation in species. A vast chasm divides these giants from the rain-maker who pours water to produce rainfall for his tribe, but the thought-processes of the man who first hit upon the idea of this ritual and theirs do have some basic elements in common. Moreover, certain primitive aspects of thinking, a remnant of the earlier childish developmental stage as described by Piaget, persist at least as a peripheral feature of the thinking of the creative scientist. A good example of this is given by a physicist:

There exists a law, known as Steinbeck's Principle, which states that an arc is not hotter than it can help being. This anthropomorphic language comes easily to those how have worked much with gas discharges. They are used to looking at an electric discharge as something like a living being, which *wants* to keep alive. [8]

The major difference between scientific thought and other kinds which shade imperceptibly into superstition is not in the initial weaving of patterns, but in the obligation imposed by the scientific ethos to verify the products of thinking by well-established methods linking it to empirical phenomena. This means that the scientist usually tries to go beyond the mere discovery of a connexion between two phenomena, and endeavours also to elucidate the intervening processes that mediate between antecedent and consequent. This has been most successfully achieved in the physical sciences, followed by the biological ones. It is far more difficult in a field like medicine, which has to deal with an exceedingly complex organism as a totality, and many of the intervening processes remain obscure. For instance Wagner-Jauregg noted that fever, being probably a manifestation of the body's struggle against disease, can be beneficial as long as it remains moderate; and he observed that it often led to the improvement of already existing ailments. Hence he hit upon the notion of producing fever in patients suffering from mental disease, with such gratifying results that he was awarded the Nobel prize; but it is still not known what precisely happens, either through fever or the other methods subsequently developed on the same principle. Many aspects of medicine are confined to empirically established relationships whose theoretical rationale is so far unknown or disputed, and because of urgent practical needs treatment cannot be denied or postponed to such time as such issues are resolved. The exacting standards of theoretically founded science cannot be rigidly adhered to, and this leaves medicine more vulnerable to unorthodox or even superstitious ideas. Analogies and similarities are exploited, honestly and dishonestly, without regard for empirical verification. Thus a French doctor related that he once happened to compare an atlas of the sky with an atlas of the brain; and how forcibly he was struck by the identical arrangement of the cells of the cortex and the stars in the galaxy. This led to his rediscovery of the human body as both the micro-image and the symbol of the cosmos, and he wrote a number of highly successful books on health and the secrets of the body. This is a case of analogy run wild, comparable with many systems prevalent before the range of undisciplined speculation was curbed by the impact of the scientific revolution.

The search for order, regularity and meaning is a general characteristic of human thought processes. It is one of our salient modes of adaptation to an ever-changing world. This does not mean, of course, that it is necessarily always functional and beneficial; on the contrary, I would suggest that in one of its aspects superstition is part of the price we pay, an inevitable by-product of the constant scanning for patterns in which we are engaged. Apart from this, there are other ways in which super- stition can be viewed in an evolutionary perspective. A geneticist[9] has pointed out that if it supports a social norm beneficial to a human group, superstition may have positive survival value. Again, the famous ethologist Konrad Lorenz[10] has put forward a biologically oriented theory linking habit, ritual and magic. He started with the observation that a young greylag goose, having deviated from a long-established habit, exhibited clear signs of acute fear relieved only by going again through the habitual motions. Lorenz attempted to show, albeit in a somewhat anec- dotal manner, that such responses are also found in humans. For instance, he described how he himself after regularly travelling along a particular route experienced anxiety when changing to another one. This account appears to me rather over-simplified, since it has been pointed out in Chapter 8 that men do not strive for complete regularity and predictability – indeed such a state would soon become intolerable; and one could easily quote contrary instances, such as the fact that walkers usually prefer to return by a different path. While Lorenz there- fore over-extends his interpretation, his main point is probably valid in the particular circumstances indicated by my italics in the quotation that follows:

All these phenomena [i.e. magical rituals of various kinds] are related. They have a common root in behaviour mechanism whose species- preserving function is obvious; *for a living being lacking insight into the relation between causes and effects* it must be extremely useful to cling to a behaviour pattern which has once or many times proved to achieve its aim, and to have done so without danger. If one does not know which details of the whole performance are essential for its success as well as for its safety, it is best to cling to them all with slavish exactitude. The principle, 'You never know what might happen if you don't' is fully expressed in such superstitions. (p. 60.)

This of course links up directly with the theories of Skinner on superstition as a conditioned response, which were examined in Chapter 5.

Lastly, in situations of acute danger or distress, usually involving excessive uncertainty, superstition is particularly likely to come to the fore. This may represent in some degree a regression to more infantile emotional attitudes as described by Freud, or a reversion to ideas and beliefs acquired during early emotional learning which remain latent under ordinary circumstances. On the other hand, as has already been suggested, superstition may at the same time serve the positive function of giving the person at least the feeling of having some control; although illusory, this may well help to preserve the integrity of the personality. Such phenomena have often been reported in crisis situations. For instance, when a volcanic eruption occurred in Hawaii in 1955, even highly educated and prominent citizens took part in such activities as throwing offerings to the volcano goddess into the lava flow.[11] One of the vicissitudes of human life which has all the ingredients conducive to superstition is disease; it often strikes suddenly without warning, was little understood in the past, and often involves emotional stress. Hence it is not surprising that everywhere superstitious beliefs and practices are particularly prevalent in this sphere; this applies even to modern industrial societies in relation to disorders not readily amenable to orthodox treatment. The obscurity of the causal relationships involved, together with the existence of the quasi-magical *placebo* effect, opens the door to all kinds of irrational and often fraudulent 'cures', eagerly sought after even by people who prior to their affliction seemed in no way superstitious. Given the appropriate circumstances, probably most of us, however much we pride ourselves on our rationality, are liable to succumb.

The burden of the thesis developed here is that superstition, far from being odd and abnormal as it is often thought to be, is in fact intimately bound up with our fundamental modes of thinking, feeling and generally responding to our environment. The current 'enlightened' attitude to superstition which purports to discern its imminent demise, aided by education, has its roots in the intellectualist optimism of the nineteenth century. This gave rise to an expectation that in due course the advancement of science would conquer the twin evils of illness and superstition, leading to a race of fit and rational supermen. Today we realize that perfect health is an unattainable ideal, because the very genetic variability which ensures our biological adaptation entails continued vulnerability to attack by micro-organisms; and the latter in turn possess the built-in variability enabling them to develop resistance against our means of destroying them. Moreover, the advance of medicine itself has produced a new crop of so-called iatrogenic diseases. Similarly, the advances of science have been accompanied by growth of new kinds of superstitions.[12] The inherent limitations in our powers to combat disease are now well understood, but many people continue to cherish the illusion that superstition is gradually fading away.

All this of course does not imply that we must resign ourselves to passivity. Just as doctors are not deterred from the fight against disease by the knowledge that there can be no ultimate victory, so educators need not be discouraged from their efforts to wean men away from harmful or even useless superstitions. But as David Hume said long ago, the propensity can never be eradicated because, paradoxically, it is an integral part of the adaptive mechanisms without which humanity would be unable to survive.

REFERENCES

1 G. W. Allport, *Personality*, New York: Holt Rinehart, 1937.
2 *Personality and the Behavior Disorders*, vol. I, New York: Ronald, 1944.
3 T. W. Adorno, E. Frenkel-Brunswik, D. J. Levinson and N. Sanford, *The Authoritarian Personality*, New York: Harper, 1950.
4 Julian B. Rotter, 'Generalized expectancies for internal versus external control of reinforcement', *Psychological Monograph* No. 609, 1966.
5 C. Zucker, *Psychologie de la Superstition*, Paris: Payot, 1952.
6 Brock Chisholme, 'Future of the Mind', in G. Wolstenholme (ed.), *Man and his Future*, London: Churchill, 1963.
7 See entry under 'Effect on superstitious beliefs' in C. W. Harris (ed.), *Encyclopaedia of Education*, 3rd edn, New York: Macmillan, 1960.
8 Dennis Gabor, 'Inventing the Future', *Encounter*, May 1960, p. 4.
9 Kenneth Mather, *Human Diversity*, Edinburgh: Oliver & Boyd, 1964.
10 *On Aggression*, Methuen, 1966.
11 R. Lachman and W. J. Bonk, 'Behavior and beliefs during the recent volcanic eruption at Kapoho, Hawaii', *Science*, 1960, 131, pp. 1095–6.
12 See for instance Martin Gardener (*Fads and Fallacies in the Name of Science*, New York: Dover, 1957).

Index of Names

Index of Subjects

More about Penguins and Pelicans

Penguinews, which appears every month, contains details of all the new books issued by Penguins as they are published. From time to time it is supplemented by *Penguins in Print*, which is a complete list of all books published by Penguins which are in print. (There are well over three thousand of these.)

A specimen copy of *Penguinews* will be sent to you free on request, and you can become a subscriber for the price of the postage. For a year's issues (including the complete lists) please send 4s. if you live in the United Kingdom, or 8s. if you live elsewhere. Just write to Dept EP, Penguin Books Ltd, Harmondsworth, Middlesex, enclosing a cheque or postal order, and your name will be added to the mailing list.

Some other psychology books published by Penguins are described on the following pages.

Note: *Penguinews* and *Penguins in Print* are not available in the U.S.A. or Canada

The Psychology of Childhood and Adolescence

C. I. SANDSTRÖM

In this concise study of the processes of growing up Professor Sandström has produced a book which, although it is perfectly suited to the initial needs of university students and teachers in training, will appeal almost as much to parents and ordinary readers. His text covers the whole story of human physical and mental growth from conception to puberty.

Outlining the scope and history of developmental psychology, Professor Sandström goes on to detail the stages of growth in the womb, during the months after birth, and (year by year) up to the age of ten. There follow chapters on physical development, learning and perception, motivation, language and thought, intelligence, the emotions, social adjustment, and personality. The special conditions of puberty and of schooling are handled in the final chapters.

Throughout this masterly study the author necessarily refers to 'norms of development': these neatly represent the average stages of growing up, but (as Professor Mace comments in his introduction) they must only be applied to individual children with caution.

The Psychology of Human Ageing

D. B. BROMLEY

Infant and adolescent psychology have been very thoroughly explored: but the study of ageing lags behind.

A gerontologist, who is scientific adviser in this field to the Medical Research Council, fills a gap in the literature of psychology with this new introduction to human ageing and its mental effects. Dealing with the course of life from maturity onwards, Dr Bromley examines many biological and social effects of human ageing; personality and adjustment; mental disorders in adult life and old age; age changes in the organization of occupational and skilled performance; adult intelligence; and age changes in intellectual, social, and other achievements. A final section on method in the study of ageing makes this book an important contribution for the student of psychology as well as the layman.

The Psychology of
Interpersonal Behaviour

MICHAEL ARGYLE

Looks, gestures, and tones of voice may be powerful factors when people meet. Moreover these rapid and subtle messages are highly co-ordinated.

Experimental techniques have recently been developed for studying the minutiae of social behaviour scientifically: these are described here by a social pscyhologist. The study of social interaction demands a 'language' of its own, to which Michael Argyle supplies a clear key. But the reader will not be slow to grasp that 'the motivation of social interaction', 'the synchronization of styles of behaviour' between two or more people, and 'the presentation of a self-image' refer to things we encounter every day.

Certain specific skills, such as interviewing, group leadership, public speaking, and even child-rearing, are discussed in the light of the latest research, and the author devotes a good deal of space to mental health and to training in social skill.
His outline of what amounts to a break-through in psychological analysis makes this a book which the student of psychology may well find indispensable; and the relevance of his material to everyday life offers irresistible reading to the plain man.

The Psychology of Learning

ROBERT BORGER AND A. E. M. SEABORNE

Only a small part of learning takes place in schools. Just as a child learns to walk, talk, and handle things without the help of trained teachers, so industrial skills are normally acquired by imitation and practice. Learning, in fact, takes place all the time, without anyone setting out either to learn or to teach.

Two psychologists discuss in this Pelican the laws which seem to govern the process of learning in its widest sense. The theories and models which have been based on simple learning situations are their first consideration: but they also provide a thorough survey of programmed learning techniques and the newer developments in the formal teaching of schools and universities.

Those in the front line of education are perhaps only just beginning to pay systematic attention to psychological studies of learning. With the view it opens up of the whole field of human and animal learning, this book can be of fundamental assistance to them.

The Psychology of Perception

M. D. VERNON

When we look at the world with our eyes, do we see it as it
really is? In this authoritative study the Professor of
Psychology at the University of Reading shows how, behind
the retina of the eye, many more fallible mental processes
cause errors and inconsistencies to creep into our perceptions.
Here is a non-technical outline of the psychological processes
which have been shown to be involved in our visual
perceptions of things around us. These perceptions of shape,
colour, movement, and space develop gradually from infancy
upwards. Finally this book, which is based on over thirty
years of psychological research at Cambridge and elsewhere,
shows how the perceptions of different people are not always
alike: they vary with attention, interest and individual
personality factors.

The Psychology of Play

SUSANNA MILLAR

The term 'play' has long been a linguistic waste-paper basket for behaviour which looks voluntary but seems to have no biological or social use. What counts as 'play'? What explanations have been given for it, and how far are they adequate? Why do children and the young of many animal species play? To answer such questions Susanna Millar here discusses psychological theories about play and reviews observational and experimental studies of the play of animals of different evolutionary development, of children at different ages, in different cultures, and in therapy. She relates different forms of play to a number of underlying behavioural mechanisms which modern methods of experimental psychology are beginning to uncover. Susanna Millar argues that play is behaviour which looks paradoxical, but has a variety of biological functions related to childhood and development and other specific conditions.